WEAPONS TRAINING

FOR

SPIRITUAL WARFARE

AND

FRONTLINE MINISTRY

A GUIDE TO WINNING BATTLES
IN THE SPIRIT REALM

DAVID ALLAN JACQUES

WESTBOW
PRESS®
A DIVISION OF THOMAS NELSON
& ZONDERVAN

WestBow Press books may be ordered through booksellers or by contacting:

WestBow Press
A Division of Thomas Nelson & Zondervan
1663 Liberty Drive
Bloomington, IN 47403
www.westbowpress.com
1 (866) 928-1240

Because of the dynamic nature of the Internet, any web addresses or
links contained in this book may have changed since publication and
may no longer be valid. The views expressed in this work are solely those
of the author and do not necessarily reflect the views of the publisher,
and the publisher hereby disclaims any responsibility for them.

Any people depicted in stock imagery provided by Thinkstock are
models, and such images are being used for illustrative purposes only.
Certain stock imagery © Thinkstock.

ISBN: 978-1-4908-5498-4 (sc)
ISBN: 978-1-4908-5497-7 (hc)
ISBN: 978-1-4908-5499-1 (e)

Library of Congress Control Number: 2014917785

Print information available on the last page.

WestBow Press rev. date: 03/18/2020

WARNING!

Don't read *Weapon's Training for Spiritual Warfare and Frontline Ministry* if you want to maintain the status quo! It may turn your world upside down by challenging the way you have always seen things!

Spiritual Warfare is a very vague and nebulous term in many circles of Christendom. Many believers talk about it but don't really know what it is or how to successfully engage in it. Some are even afraid of or at least uncomfortable with the subject.

My purpose for *Weapons Training for Spiritual Warfare and Frontline Ministry* is to arm the Christian with a working knowledge of how to engage our enemy in battle successfully, taking ground away from the demonic and bringing light into places previously occupied by darkness.

God wants more than anything to see His church (His bride) walk in purity and in victory, so I give the believer in Christ a working knowledge of the various spiritual weapons made available to them. I will teach you how to effectively employ these weapons. I will train you for war, so that you might gain the victory in your walk with God, win the lost out of darkness, and effectively destroy the works of the devil!

In this way you will begin to truly experience kingdom reality and dominion over the demonic. Moreover, you will start to be the change agent in your sphere of influence as God uses you to advance His kingdom....This will bring breakthrough in your life and in the lives of others as you learn *Weapons Training for Spiritual Warfare and Frontline Ministry.*

"For though we walk in the flesh, we do not war according to the flesh, for the weapons of our warfare are not of the flesh, but divinely powerful for the destruction of fortresses. We are destroying speculations and every lofty thing raised up against the knowledge of God..."
2 Corinthians 10:3-5
NASB

Edited by
Teresa Giovati Archer
teresapearl@yahoo.com

I wish to give a special thanks to Teresa
Giovati Archer for editing.
Her comments and suggestions were invaluable. She
clearly made this a better and more readable book.

Dedication

I want to thank the following people for their contributions to my life and ministry. To my dad and mom, thank you for all that you invested in me and for helping me become the man that I am today. I love you both dearly.

To Lori, my precious wife; she is truly a gift of God. Her gentle, quiet spirit has been an encouragement to me time and time again. This may seem like a cliché, but the truth is this book would not have been written without her help. Her patience with my time commitments and her thoughtful advice have been invaluable.

To my son and daughter, Alex and Nicollette, two gifts from the Lord that he continues to use in my spiritual development as a man and as a parent.

To Jeffrey and Katy Barsch and Dan Burke from the Ventura Healing Rooms for their mentorship and modeling a lifestyle that clearly displays spiritual power in the context of God's love. Their friendship enabled me to embrace extreme possibilities.

To David and Karen Clatterbuck who have been like a father and mother to me. They are the best in-laws any man could have.

To the late John Wimber of Anaheim Vineyard Christian Fellowship for his teaching and indirect influence on the lives of so many, including my own.

To Steve Hampton and all my friends who have helped me step into my destiny. The Lord bless you all as we continue to embrace the greatest of all adventures.

CONTENTS

PROLOGUE

In my post college years, I was participating in a weekly prayer ministry when I met her. Wendy (not her real name) was desperate, tormented and visibly shaken. She had come for help and had nowhere else to turn. When I asked her what the problem was, she was hesitant to say anything. I explained that in order to help her I would need a little more to go on. Finally, she said through her tears, "I'm being raped."

"By who?" I asked. She began to sob as she said, "Right now! I am being raped right this moment!" Wendy went on to explain that for several months she had not been able to sleep or function normally. She would, for example, try to sleep in her bed, and would begin to experience all the physical sensations of being raped. This would happen whether she was in the market doing her shopping or at work. As a result she was missing more and more work and becoming more and more isolated. She went on to tell me that these episodes had increased with greater frequency. She had gone to other pastors and other churches and nobody knew how to help her. Moreover, people were even suggesting that she might be mentally ill. She assured me that she was not mentally ill and that these attacks were spiritual in nature.

Once I was sure I knew what I was dealing with, I took authority over the demon and said, "I command this tormenting spirit to cease and desist in Jesus' Name! Stop it now!" I then asked her if it had stopped, and she said it did.

As I spoke with her further, I learned that Wendy had been molested for several years as a young girl and was later very promiscuous into her teens and 20's before coming to Christ. Now in her 30's, she told me she had recently been raped by a man while visiting another country. The promiscuity of her past and the trauma of the recent event had opened a "doorway" and had given a demon a foothold in her life.

As we began to pray, I asked the Holy Spirit to show Wendy who she needed to forgive. (Unforgiveness can often bind us to our past) As God spoke to Wendy's heart, she started to remember the men who had hurt her whom she needed to forgive. As she forgave them and released them to the Lord, we also spoke each man's name before Father God, breaking and severing the soul ties created by these ungodly unions. Lastly, Wendy forgave herself; she needed to forgive the little girl inside her that had made her vulnerable. I then decreed the blood of Jesus over Wendy. I then commanded the spirit of rape and trauma to leave her, never to return. Immediately, there was visible release in Wendy's countenance. She was free.

A couple of months later I ran into Wendy who had brought another friend of hers for ministry. She was still completely free at that time. Praise God for His grace and mercy!

INTRODUCTION

It is rare that someone is as severely demonized and tormented as Wendy was. However, many people (including believers) experience some level of interference from the demonic realm even though they may not be consciously aware of it. Throughout the Bible we see the demonic exerting varying degrees of influence over people. Sometimes people are described as being merely being "troubled," like the reference in Luke 6:18 where it says that some who were **troubled** with unclean spirits were being cured. We also read in 1 Samuel16:14 that when the Spirit of the Lord departed from Saul, he began to be "tormented" by an evil spirit. This word **tormented** can also be translated "terrorized." This word seems to be descriptive of an even greater level of demonization. Moreover, we read in Luke 8:27 that Jesus encounters a man living naked among the tombs who was "possessed" with an infestation of the demonic. This **possessed** man appears to be one of the most severe cases of demonization recorded in the scriptures. Possession denotes ownership, and though demons cannot literally own anybody, we have to presume that this man was spending very little time in his right mind. So, we can see through the scriptures that there is a *spectrum of influence* that the enemy can exert if given the grounds to do so.

I believe that most often our enemy works in very subtle ways, ways that without spiritual discernment would be completely missed or overlooked. Now I'm not writing this book to foster paranoia. Nor am I seeking to get you looking for a demon under every rock. However, I have discovered that as I have journeyed with Jesus Christ, He has made me aware of various spiritual weapons that significantly improved the quality of my life when I employed them. This epiphany helped me to realize that my Christianity is for much more than salvation and church attendance, as glorious as that is! I began to realize that Christ has given us all the essential tools to walk in victory and the weapons to win the spiritual battles personally, at home, and in the workplace. I began to understand more about what was purchased for me on the cross, and all that was provided for me by Christ's resurrection. Taking possession of my "promised land" was the inspiration for this book.

We as Westernized believers tend to interpret much of what we see and experience through a very rationalistic worldview. That is to say, much of what we experience in our day-to-day lives is seen as innocuous and business-as-usual. We tend to interpret things through natural sight instead of spiritual sight. In my own personal journey through healing and deliverance I have come to realize that demonization is experienced on a spectrum. This spectrum translates into "degrees of influence." Discerning demonic influence enables us as Christians to know how to pray and to effectively wage war spiritually.

BORN INTO BATTLE

Growing up as a child I was raised Catholic. However, though I was Catholic, I did not grow up in a Christian home. That is to say, none of the substance of the Christian faith ever transferred to our family's home life. Church attendance, therefore, was an exercise. We attended Mass until my siblings and I were "confirmed." At that point, for reasons unknown to me, we stopped attending Mass. I was in junior high school at the time.

The next four years brought a lot of change to our lives. My mother was more and more preoccupied and less available emotionally. My dad began to work longer hours. My parents were drifting apart. Even my siblings started to rebel against the shift and change in our family spending more and more time away from home. My brother, who was the youngest, became the forgotten child. Eventually, my dad remarried. My family was ripped apart, and it seemed there wasn't anything I could do about it.

It was about this time that I came to Jesus Christ through a very committed and enthusiastic youth ministry of a nearby non-denominational Christian church. I attended because of the invitation of a friend, and I found the stability of this group attractive at this time in my life. After attending for several months, I accepted Jesus Christ and was baptized that same day. I was truly "born again" by the Spirit of God. The impact on my life was dramatic, and though I knew nothing about spiritual warfare at the time, I immediately discerned the obvious differences in atmospheres. This church, for example, seemed filled with joy and peace. I was in the honeymoon period of my Christianity, and it was glorious! I fell in love with God and the church. I spent as much time there as possible. It felt so stable, sound, and safe.

Conversely, I would go home and find myself enveloped in darkness. The darkness was palpable. Home was chaotic, unpredictable, and depressing. My dad was spending more time away from home, and my mother struggling with his absence. She had been a stay-at-home mother throughout her marriage to my dad. After he left, she began to feel desperate and afraid. (At the time, I didn't know mother was desperate and afraid). There were always strangers in our house from the local pub that my mother had invited home to continue their "celebrations". Home for me, however, was not a happy place.

I attempted many times to share the gospel with my family members but was ineffective. Hostility raged between my siblings and me because of past hurts. My mother, plagued with guilt, could not hear what I had to say. My dad was just angry that I wasn't attending "the right church". Not feeling equipped to deal with all the emotional turmoil, after high school I left and joined the Marine Corps.

> *"Our struggle (battle) is not against flesh and blood, but against rulers, against powers, against the world forces of this darkness, against the spiritual forces of wickedness in the heavenly places"*
> Ephesians 6:12 NASB

It wasn't until years later that I began to understand the unseen forces that raged within my family and the home that I grew up in. The battle against my family and me began long before I came to Christ. It came through unseen doorways, spiritual portals, secret sins, and generational curses handed down from generations past. Demonic spirits had long established fortresses and strongholds through a network of lies. Forces of evil had laid spiritual land mines in our lives, and we were unaware of it. The fact is...I was born into a battle of which I was completely oblivious to and lacked the weapons to fight.

When I was in the Marine Corps, I studied and trained for war. I had to learn hand-to-hand combat. I was expected to learn how to handle an M-16 and eventually earned four awards as an expert rifleman. I learned to handle a bayonet, rig claymore mines, and use numerous other weapons. Most importantly, we had to learn how to gain the tactical advantage and fight as a unit.

To send men out to fight a war without proper weapons training would be to set them up for sure defeat. Yet too often the church sends Christians out into the world (sometimes the mission field) armed with only the ABC's of the faith. As a result, many Christians become discouraged, broken, defeated, and at best, only marginally effective.

> *"Therefore leaving the elementary teaching of Christ let us press on to maturity, not laying again a foundation of repentance from dead works and of faith toward God, and of instruction about...the resurrection of the dead and eternal judgment."*
>
> Hebrews 6:1-2 NASB

PURPOSE OF THIS BOOK

The book you hold in your hands was forged by my journey through the fire of my own healing and deliverance. As I have spent many years helping others through their personal journeys toward healing and freedom, I have discovered a number of spiritual weapons that are available through the cross and the resurrection of Jesus Christ. Moreover, these weapons began to have great and practical relevance in my day-to-day life, both in ministry and in my workplace. As

I began to experience more victory in my personal life, I was simultaneously noticing many defeated and struggling Christians around me. I saw that many Christians were unaware of all the weapons and tools that are available to them in this spiritual war. It became immediately obvious to me that many believers did not even know they were in a war. Moreover, many didn't understand their identity and the authority and power made available to them through the cross and the resurrection of Jesus Christ. It was then that I felt moved to write this book. The Lord has taught me how to effectively shut down the demonic in the various spheres of my life; it is the acquisition of these spiritual weapons and my successful experience with them that I hope to impart to you.

One of the first places I began to experience the practicality of spiritual warfare was in my own marriage and family. With my kids, for example, conflicts, arguing, and sibling rivalry all but died out or became significantly muted in comparison. I also began to see my workplace affected as well, as I began to employ some of these spiritual weapons.

I work as one of the security officers at the courthouse in my town. My work-place, previously a hostile work environment, began to change almost immediately. As I began learning how to effectively limit demonic activity in my workplace, I immediately began to notice changes in my work environment. This experience began to open my eyes to just how much influence these unseen forces have in our day-to-day lives and how we can begin to defeat them.

> *"Or how can anyone enter the strong man's house and carry off his property, unless he first binds the strong man? And then he will plunder his house."*
> Matthew 12:29 NASB

"Spiritual Warfare" is a very vague and nebulous term in many circles of Christendom. It is also considered to be a very broad topic. Many believers talk about it but don't really know what it is or how to successfully engage in it. Some are even afraid of or at least uncomfortable with the subject. My purpose is that this book will arm the Christian with a working knowledge of how to engage our enemy in battle successfully, taking ground away from the demonic realm and bringing light into places previously occupied by darkness. God wants more than anything to see His church (His bride) walk in purity and in victory, so I give the believer in Christ a working knowledge of the various spiritual weapons made available to them. I will teach you how to effectively employ these weapons. I will train you for war so that you can gain the victory in your walk with God, win the lost out of darkness, and effectively destroy the works of the devil! In this way you will begin to truly experience kingdom reality and dominion over the demonic. Moreover, you will start to be the change agent in your sphere of influence as God uses you to advance His kingdom. This will bring breakthrough in your life and in the lives of others. However, this happens only as you learn to walk in *spiritual authority*, the next issue I will address.

CHAPTER 1

SPIRITUAL AUTHORITY

*"Behold, I have given you authority to tread on
serpents and scorpions, and over all the power
of the enemy, and nothing will injure you."*
Luke 10:19 NASB

Some Christians see "The Wizard of Oz" (the original movie) as a prophetic picture of the church, and believe that it was actually inspired by the Holy Spirit. It's been suggested that the characters in the movie represent different sides or expressions of the church. For example, the Tin-Man illustrates that dimension of the church which tends to be rigid with little passion. The Tin-Man church is all head and no heart. It's a rigid church. On the other hand, the Scarecrow illustrates that part of the church which has lots of heart and passion, but little knowledge. Lack of understanding causes him to fall apart when challenged. When the enemy intensifies his attack, the scarecrow runs scared. The Cowardly Lion is characterized by fear. He lacks clear identity, not knowing who he is or his place in the world. He may attempt to act brave, but not really believing in who he is, the cowardly lion church runs away, terrified by evil. Always in a defensive posture, this church is afraid of stepping out in faith and taking risks. They fear being deceived, and they fear any manifestations of the Holy Spirit. Dorothy ties this metaphor all together. Not realizing what gift she has received in those ruby red slippers, she remains unaware of the power and authority that she has over the wicked witch, and she runs scared, too.

I'm not going to argue whether or not this movie is prophetic. I simply want to use it as a helpful tool to illustrate spiritual authority. I do believe that in many ways, "The Wizard of Oz" accurately mirrors the church today. The church runs frightened by the devil because she lacks understanding of who she is, what she's been given, and the power and authority she has over the enemy. Her insecurity and rigidity make her vulnerable to lies and make her afraid of spiritual power. Consequently, she has no idea of her true mission in the world or the resources she has at her disposal.

WHERE AUTHORITY COMES FROM

The resurrection of Jesus provided us with one of the most powerful and effective spiritual weapons of warfare the church will ever possess. This weapon is our authority in Christ. Authority comes from three things: position, commission, and power. Though power is a separate entity, there is a close relationship between power and authority. No job illustrates this more clearly than that of a police officer. A police officer is a person given a **position** of authority. That authority is made evident to the public by his uniform. The badge on his uniform represents the city or state that has authorized the officer's **commission** to protect and serve. The officer's training and utility belt typically equips him with a gun, a nightstick, and mace spray. This gives the officer multiple levels of force and the **power** to enforce the state and municipal laws of the land.

In a similar manner, the disciple of Jesus Christ has been given spiritual authority to enforce the rule and reign of Christ over the demonic realm. The disciple of Jesus is, therefore, given a **position** of authority. That position comes out of our identity in Christ.

OUR IDENTITY IN CHRIST

It's important to know that your identity in Christ is foundational to operating in spiritual authority. According to God's word, we are each members of a royal priesthood, a holy nation, a people belonging to God (1 Peter 2:9). That means you are royalty. Our Father has made us co-heirs with Christ, and He has raised us up and seated us with Christ in heavenly places (Ephesians 2:6). We are sons and daughters of the King of all kings (2 Cor. 10:18). We have the Spirit of adoption! We can call God our Abba, Daddy, or Father! (Romans 8:16) Do you realize what this means?! It means that we are **Princes and Princesses.** Not fairy tale princes and princesses, but **real** ones! God has made us to be **kings and queens** to rule and reign in His stead! We are royalty, and what does royalty do? Royalty rules and reigns! This means that as disciples of Jesus we have **position.** We have a special relationship with our Father, the King of kings. NOW, let the reality of that truth sink into your head for a moment.

This truth has serious ramifications in regards to spiritual warfare and effectiveness in ministry, not to mention life in general. When believers know who they are, darkness trembles. Unfortunately, like the Cowardly Lion in the Wizard of Oz who keeps singing, *"IF I were king of the forest!,"* many Christians don't believe. You see, truth be told, the Cowardly Lion *was* the king of the forest. He just didn't believe it! So, he lived in fear, cowering every time the witch came by. Sadly, many Christians live defeated and in fear for the same reasons. They simply do not know who they are. Becoming established in your identity in Christ is a must to exercise spiritual authority and to embrace our commission.

OUR COMMISSION

After successful completion of an academy, police recruits take an oath with their department to protect, serve, and enforce the laws of the land. It is at this point that they are *commissioned* as police officers and given the powers of arrest.

God's commission to mankind began in the garden. God made the garden of Eden to be the most ideal place for man and woman. We can only imagine what it was like. It must have featured all the glory and splendor of God's creation. It must have had the perfect conditions and been a land of plenty.

We don't know what it was like outside the boundaries of the garden. We can only speculate. However, we do know that prior to the creation of mankind; Satan had occupied the earth for an unknown period of time. This leads me to believe that creation outside the garden was untamed and somewhat corrupted. So, God created Adam and Eve and put them in the garden to steward His creation. It was then that God commissioned them saying, *"Be fruitful and multiply and fill the earth and subdue it; and rule....over every living thing"* (Genesis 1:28 NASB). In other words, God gave mankind authority to bring the rest of creation into conformity with the garden, God's perfect model for creation.

Mankind became God's custodians over creation to rule and reign in His stead. They were to operate and steward the land as a people in intimate fellowship with Him. As such, they were to be fruitful, multiply, and fill the earth by bringing God's rule over the rest of creation and throughout the earth. They were intended to bring the entire earth back under God's order and influence.

Beyond the Garden, creation had been corrupted by Satan and his minions. Man, however, had authority over both Satan and creation. Over time, as men and women began to populate the earth, their offspring would venture out and remodel the earth after God's design in the Garden. They were designed to bring God's influence to the farthest corners of creation as they remained in close and intimate relationship with Him. The earth would eventually be subdued by mankind and be made into the likeness of the Garden of Eden. Idyllic conditions would exist with men and women in close relationship to God. God, in turn, would rule the earth through His children by having delegated His authority to them.

We all know the rest of the story. Adam and Eve fell. Being deceived by the serpent, they both sinned and forfeited what God had entrusted to them. The earth came under the devil's influence. Evil increased as mankind came into the bondage of sin and agreement with the enemy.

Thankfully, that is not the end of the story. Jesus Christ, God incarnate, came back to earth to succeed where Adam failed. The death, burial and resurrection of Jesus bought back for us what man had lost and reversed the curse of Adam for those who would believe. Then in Matthew 28:18-19,

Christ re-commissions the disciples saying, *"All authority has been given to me in heaven and on earth. Go therefore* (remember He transferred His authority to His disciples in Luke 10:19) *and make disciples* (multiply)....*Teaching them to do all that I commanded you; and lo, I am with you always, even to the end of the age."*

Now, what did Jesus teach and command the disciples to do? He taught many things, but primarily three things were most obvious: to proclaim the gospel of the kingdom of God, to heal the sick, and to cast out demons. This is how God intends His church to subdue the earth. We as believers have been commissioned by God to destroy the works of the devil. (Luke 9:1-2, 10:1, 17-19.)

By shedding His blood on the cross and rising from the dead, Christ succeeded where man had failed, and He reversed the curse of Adam. Then Christ re-commissioned mankind to subdue the earth with God's influence (Matthew 28:18-20 and in Mark 16:15-18). God brought man back full circle to His original plan, in which He told Adam and Eve subdue the earth. We are to do this by following Christ's example to destroy the works of the devil and to establish the rule and reign of God's kingdom as His people. The "kingdom of God" is literally the rule and reign of Christ. Jesus completely reinstated everything man had lost!

Before, Satan had corrupted the earth with sin and all forms of evil, afflictions, maladies, disease, sicknesses, plagues, poverty, and all forms of destruction and disasters that would be considered natural. Now man has been re-commissioned with God's delegated authority to rule and reign in His stead by imposing the rule of Christ's kingdom over darkness. We, as the Church, are to police the earth by enforcing the rule and reign of Christ over spiritual darkness and the demonic realm.

We do this by shutting down demonic influence, healing the sick, delivering those who are afflicted and in bondage, and bringing light where there is darkness.

Police officers are confident in exercising authority. They know that as long as they operate within the legal boundaries of their jurisdiction they can enforce the law, and they will be backed by the city or state that commissioned them to perform their duty. It works the same way in spirit realms.

Christians who desire to operate effectively must know their commission and be confident in their authority in Christ. We as believers are backed by the King of heaven to enforce Christ's rule and reign over darkness. This reality must be the conviction of every believer who desires to be an effective man or woman of God. Part of being effective involves exercising spiritual power when appropriate. The power of God, though different and separate from spiritual authority, is still an essential part of it. Spiritual power is the subject I want to address next in relation to the exercise of spiritual authority.

POWER OF GOD

The Power of God is such a broad topic that one could devote a whole book to the subject. For my purposes in addressing this subject, I will attempt to answer three questions: 1) Why does the believer need the power of God? 2) What role does spiritual power play in the exercise of spiritual authority? 3) How does one acquire spiritual power? Now, I will share part of my story with you.

I had been a "born-again" believer in Jesus Christ for six years before I ever experienced the power of God. I considered my conversion to be fairly radical, like flipping on a light switch or like seeing the world in black and white and then, all of a sudden, seeing it in color. I began talking to everyone I knew about Jesus. My enthusiasm and zeal seemed to repel most of the people I knew, including (and especially) my parents. They were not at all ready to have a preacher in the family, least of all to have someone preaching to *them*. I must admit, I was not very mature or discerning regarding other people. Nor was I very sensitive to the feelings of others. I had some blind spots and a lot of dysfunction in my own life that I was unaware of at the time. And though I was saved, I had not yet dealt with my demons. The fact was, I didn't even know a Christian could have a demon.

I had been raised in a household that, from the outside, seemed very much like a normal middle class family. This, of course, was not the case. At home I often experienced an angry, hyper-critical, and verbally abusive environment. Alcohol addiction was also prevalent. This combination of dysfunction served to create a very unstable home life. I remember feeling depressed, fearful, and very angry. I was a young teen at this time, and I would often seek escape to a friend's house where we would indulge ourselves in his dad's secret stash of pornography. It would be years later before I came to realize the profound impact my home life had had on me. When I turned 20 years old, I joined the Marine Corps, partly to escape. I would later learn that children raised in addictive and abusive homes often cope by taking on a particular role in their family of origin. This, in turn, leads to a lack of identity and emotional development. I knew nothing of the dynamics in my family at the time. I simply wanted to get away from a painful situation.

When I was 24 years old, it was my last year in the military, and I was dating a girl I had met at church. I fell fast and hard for this gal, and her feelings were mutual. I had been overseas on a tour of the South Pacific, and we had been corresponding by mail. When I returned and we resumed dating again, I started noticing a growing fear inside me. I would try to shrug it off, but it just continued to grow more intense over time. The fear was that she would one day stop loving me and eventually reject me. I was fearing abandonment, which was something I had experienced emotionally time and time again as a child. Growing up, it wasn't uncommon that I would come home from school with no one emotionally available. On a number of occasions I would come home and find a family member passed out on the carpet. In those moments, as a child, all I could think was, *my mother is gone, and what am I going to do now?* With each similar experience, the fear just continued to grow. Later, as an adult, when I began dating this young woman, all that fear that I had somehow locked away came roaring back, and it was overwhelming. She had started college and was involved in a volleyball league. I was not able to cope with the increasing demands on her time with academics and extra-curricular activities, so I broke off the relationship. It was a desperate act of manipulation and coercion. It came from extreme immaturity and insecurity, and I hurt her deeply. Moreover, the plan backfired. She, being much healthier than I, refused to risk being hurt again. My worst fear was realized; the relationship ended.

Ironically, I had sensed a call into ministry while in the Marine Corps, so after my last year in the service I started my education at a Christian college in Fullerton, California. It was my sophomore year of Bible College, and I was still hurting and feeling very broken. I was still dealing with the pain from my break- up. It was at this time that I met a man on campus by the name of Steve Hampton. Steve had pastored a Vineyard Church in Hawaii and was finishing his last year of Bible College. I didn't even know about the Vineyard. It was 1989, and I had been attending Calvary Chapel in Costa Mesa. I was attending different Bible studies four to five nights a week in addition to my college studies. I was desperately looking for the remedy to my brokenness, and I thought if I just filled myself with enough Bible knowledge it would somehow fix me. It didn't. I just became more cynical.

I was attending college, living in the dorms, and trying to pay my own way through school. I had gotten a job working campus security to pay for my dormitory. This meant that when I worked I spent my evenings making sure all the classrooms were locked after night classes finished.

Steve Hampton was like no man I had ever met before. He was an anointed worshipper and guitarist, but what was even more striking to me was the way Steve was able to hear the voice of God. Over the course of the semester He had gathered a small group of us on campus. We made a habit of worshipping together in his dorm room at the end of the day. Late one night, when the dorms were locked down, we all wanted to worship together. Since I was entrusted with the keys to the school classrooms, I decided to open up one of the furthest classrooms away from the dorms so as to avoid disturbing anybody. Inside we all sat in front of the classroom on the carpet in a semi-circle with our legs crossed as Steve led us in song. About twenty minutes into the worship, Steve stopped and said something to the group that would change my life forever. He said, *"God just spoke to me, and He told me that He would like all of you to know Him in a very special way. Now, hold your hands out like you are about to receive something."* So, we did. Then Steve said, *"Holy Spirit, come."*

As we sat there waiting in silence, my body began to move involuntarily back and forth. I even opened my eyes to see who was touching me. There were women sitting on both sides of me and neither one of them were touching or leaning on me in any way.

I said, "Steve, I'm moving! What's going on?" Steve said, "Relax. That's the Holy Spirit. The Holy Spirit comes in waves." At that point I just kept thinking where in scripture does it say the Holy Spirit comes in waves? Then I remembered that Jesus often compared the Spirit to water...living water. Steve then began going around the group praying for each of us to receive the gift of healing.

That event came and went, and I was still very broken, but what began to take place over the course of that year was a series of powerful visitations of the Holy Spirit. I would be sitting at my desk, and the Spirit of the Lord would begin to move me like He did in that classroom. That summer I began to complete my pastoral internship at Long Beach Christian Church, and I was housesitting for some folks at the church who were out of town. One night while I was reading, the Spirit of the Lord began to stir me. So, I put down my book and sat down on the floor as I had done before in that classroom. The Spirit's movement continued. I began to ask for more of God. I kept saying, "More Lord! More Lord!" Each time I asked Him for more, He came stronger and stronger as jolts of raw power began coursing through my body. At one point it felt like ten thousand volts going through my body! My body was bouncing two feet off the ground. That night I hardly slept as my body kept convulsing under the power. And though I had hardly slept, I was completely refreshed the next morning.

The nights following, the power continued to come. I would stay awake all night talking to Him. It was a glorious period. By the end of Summer I knew God was bringing me into a new season. It was a season of personal healing. As time went on, God began to bring me through what I could only describe as a personality meltdown. Once again, I began to revisit all the fear and the pain of my past. He was peeling back the "onion," stripping away all the false identities I had acquired in all those years while growing up. I was even experiencing torment and sleeplessness from demonic spirits, because past sins had opened doors to the enemy. Night after night I would be harassed by the demonic. I was desperate for help.

The fall semester of my junior year was starting, and I couldn't wait to see Steve. When I saw him, I told him all that I had been experiencing. He invited me to the Anaheim Vineyard, so I went. I was enthralled and caught up. Never, had I seen God as evident in a church before. I witnessed laughter, healing, tears, and deliverance amidst the glorious worship of God's people. I began getting prayer ministry at the evening services, and I joined a small group soon after. The prayer ministry was powerful as God released me from lies, shame, and a number of demonic influences. By the end of my senior year, I was completely free. God's power had set me free and had brought a degree of wholeness into my life that I had never experienced before.

I share my story to emphasize one point. Bible study alone couldn't heal me. All the theology and "sound doctrine" couldn't do it, and church alone couldn't heal me either. **It took people who could access God's power to help me.**

Now that I have shared part of my story with you, let's go back to the previous questions. 1) Why does the believer need the power of God, and 2) what role does spiritual power play in the exercise of spiritual authority?

Remember the policeman analogy? A police officer is given a **position** of authority to enforce the laws of the land and is then **commissioned** to do so. However, that positional authority would be meaningless without the **power** to back it up. Therefore, the officer is given training, a gun, a nightstick, and mace to wear on a utility belt. These weapons empower the officer to effectively enforce the law.

So, why does the believer need the power of God? We need the power of God to effectively subdue the earth, destroying the works of the devil. Christians need the power of God to enforce the kingdom rule and reign of Christ. We need spiritual power to impose the reality of heaven into places currently occupied by spiritual forces of darkness. I needed Christians who had an understanding of spiritual power to help me get healed and delivered. Without God's anointed ones, I would still be in my brokenness.

The next question is somewhat trickier to answer because there are no formulas that God follows. However, I will attempt to give it a go. So, here it goes.

How does a Christian acquire spiritual power? The simple answer is... by being hungry for it. Jesus commands us to *"Seek first the kingdom of God and His righteousness..."* (Matthew 6:33). Jesus went on to say, *"Ask, and it shall be given to you, seek and you shall find, knock and the door will be opened, for everyone who asks receives, and he who seeks finds, and to him who knocks the door will be opened"* (Matthew 7:7-8). I must emphasize the need for desperate hunger and desire for more of God in your life. It's those who hunger and thirst who will be filled. My pain and brokenness brought me to a place of desperation for God.

Also, I had sought to surround myself with men and women of God who were demonstrating evidence of God's touch on their lives. I was even willing to travel to find them. They were people who regularly prayed for healing for others. They would hear God's voice and speak into people's hearts words of life from God's heart. The friends I surrounded myself with were people who were seekers of God, always pressing in to know Him better. They were worshippers, always giving themselves to God. They were men and women of faith who would believe God for the impossible. They were not content with the status quo.

Another thing I did was open myself up to teachers who moved in miracles. The late John Wimber was the first of these prominent teachers I began learning from. Later, I began to listen to many others who moved in and demonstrated God's power in their lives. I began reading many books about anointed men and women of the past such as John G. Lake, Smith Wigglesworth, Kathryn Kulman and others. I began attending conferences by those who taught and encouraged healing ministry, and I avoided naysayers.

Again, there is no formula. However, our God is generous and an extravagant giver. Our Father delights in giving His children the kingdom. So ask, seek, and knock! Father will not delay long in answering, and it will almost certainly begin His process in bringing you to a new place that prepares you for victory over darkness.

God has given His church an arsenal of weapons to walk in victory over the devil, and to plunder the kingdom of darkness. Our authority in Jesus Christ is pivotal in the use of all our weapons in this spiritual battle. To exercise authority we must be established in our identity in Christ and know who we are. We must understand our commission and know what it is that our King has commanded us to do. And lastly, we must receive God's power to do what Jesus did. He came to be about His Father's business. Jesus came to destroy the works of the devil and to bring abundant life to the world. We must do likewise, following the same rules of engagement that Christ modeled.

CHAPTER 2

RULES OF ENGAGEMENT

"For our battle is not against flesh and blood, but against the rulers, against the powers, against the world forces of this darkness, against the spiritual forces of wickedness in the heavenly places"
Ephesians 6:12 NASB

Plural noun

Rules of Engagement:

1. A directive issued by a military authority specifying the circumstances and limitations under which forces will engage in combat with the enemy.

Before we delve into the rest of our spiritual arsenal, it is important that I first cover some rules of engagement for what is, in essence, our battlefield. Now I want to emphasize that our battle is not against people. God has called us to love by showing His compassion and understanding to the men and women we have contact with from day to day. Our fight is against the demonic, spiritual forces that often use human hosts to speak and to act on their behalf.

I believe that each city, state, and country has different kinds of principalities and powers that are unique (for the most part) to that region. I also believe that those spiritual forces will tend to manifest themselves in a number of physical ways. A Christian can discern what kind of spiritual forces dominate a region by observing these physical "outcroppings." For example, a city like Amsterdam would appear to have a principality or ruling spirit of lust or pornography dominating that region. This is evident by the number of porn shops and prostitution going on in that part of the world. Another city might have a spirit of addiction, and another, a spirit of poverty. Other ruling spirits may bring idolatry, pride or materialism to a region. A city or country could have any combination of these ruling principalities over them, and they will manifest their presence and influence through the businesses and trade that go on in them.

It was a number of years ago, armed with this knowledge, that I (notice the word "I") thought it would be a good idea to walk the streets of my town and pray **alone** against the principalities over my city. I would observe a head shop, so I would pray against the spirit of sorcery. I would see an abortion clinic, so I would pray against the spirit of murder and death. I was aware of gang violence in my town, so I would pray against the spirit of violence and addiction. I had no idea what I was doing, and so I walked up and down Main Street praying out loud, "You spirit of (fill in the blank) I bind you, and I break your power. You have no place here! Leave now in Jesus name!"

It wasn't until I woke up the next morning that I realized something was terribly wrong. The first thing I noticed was that my hands, wrists, and forearms were aching and in severe pain. Now I've never been a person who has had any kind of aches or pains. I've always been healthy and strong all my life, so I immediately connected the affliction with my activities downtown the previous day. To say that I was very concerned is an understatement. I sought immediate help from a woman at church who I knew to be a gifted intercessor. When I told her what I had been doing and the pain I was currently experiencing, she said, "Oh, you should never do that! That's outside your sphere of authority." I repented and asked if she would pray for me, so she did. She laid her hands on top of my hands and began to pray, and as she prayed, the pain immediately began to subside and left altogether. Nothing like learning things the hard way!

I share this story to illustrate that there are certain rules of engagement in spiritual warfare that we must observe just as we observe certain physical laws that govern the universe, like the law of gravity. Similar to these natural laws, there are also spiritual laws that govern the spirit realm. These spiritual laws bind the demonic to certain rules that protect the Christian. Believers get in trouble when they ignore these rules and give the enemy access or grounds to attack.

Much of this chapter has come out of my experience in spiritual warfare through trial and error. I don't claim to have all the answers, nor do I claim to be an expert. I am just a servant of Christ trying to practice my faith, and trying to be as effective as I can be in the real world. So, I pushed my limits and even crossed some boundaries on occasion, but I have learned from my mistakes. My hope is that my experience might be of some benefit to those who desire to be more victorious and more effective warriors for Christ's kingdom.

DEMONIC SANCTIONS

Sanc.tion (noun): a military or coercive measure to impel or insure compliance to a standard of behavior. (Webster's dictionary)

"Then Satan answered the Lord, 'Does Job fear God for nothing? Hast thou not made a hedge about him and his house and all that he has on every side? Thou hast blessed the work of his hands, and his possessions have increased in the land. But put forth Thy hand and touch all that he has; he will surely curse you to your face.' Then the Lord said to Satan, 'Behold all that he has is in your power, only do not put forth your hand on him. 'So Satan departed from the presence of the Lord."

Job 1:9-12 NASB

It is important to know that the demonic realm can do nothing to the believer without God's permission or our agreement. That is to say, every believer is under God's protective care. Satan and his minions are sanctioned against direct attack on the believer unless they can get Christians to sin or to come into agreement with them. The believer who resists the devil and binds him is impervious to attack when walking in authority and obedience in the grace of God.

EXCEPTIONS TO THE RULE

Now I want to qualify that statement by bringing your attention to the above passage in the book of Job. There are three things we learn in the book of Job.

1. All of God's people are under His protection and blessing.
2. Satan can do nothing without having grounds or permission.
3. *Afflictions do not always mean the believer has sinned.*

Like most rules we follow in life, there is always the exception. To qualify what I am going to say in this chapter, I want to first address statement number 3. *"Afflictions do not always mean that the believer has sinned."* According to the book of Job, believers are sometimes given seasons of testing. God alone knows the reason for the test and its length of time unless He chooses to reveal it. Tests are designed to teach, strengthen, and establish the believer. Tests, however, are the exception and not the rule.

THE RULE

The rule is that...if a believer walks with God in holiness and obedience, and resists the devil by exercising his or her spiritual authority, that person will remain under God's protection and blessing. Again, Satan and his demons are sanctioned against direct attack on the believer who walks with God. They can do nothing without permission or our cooperation.

Why do I say this? I say this because if we examine scripture in its entirety, we see a clear pattern emerge. Let's start with the children of Israel. In Deuteronomy 30, we read that the children of Israel are reminded about the covenant in Moab. The Lord reminds the people that if they obey the Lord and walk with Him with all their heart and soul, according to all his commands, He will bless them.

> *"Then the Lord your God will prosper you abundantly in all the work of your hands, in your offspring of your body, and in the offspring of your cattle, and the produce of the ground, for the Lord will again indeed rejoice over you for good, just as He rejoiced over your fathers.....See,*

> *I have set before you this day life and prosperity, and death and adversity; in that I command you today to love the Lord your God, to walk in His ways and to keep His commandments.... That you may live and multiply, and that the Lord your God may bless you in the land where you are entering to possess it.*
>
> *But if your heart turns away and you will not obey, but are drawn away to worship other gods and serve them, I declare to you today that you shall surely perish. You shall not prolong your days in the land where you are crossing the Jordan to possess it. I call heaven and earth to witness against you today, that I have set before you life and death, the blessing and the curse. So choose life in order that you may live, you and your descendents, by loving the Lord your God, by obeying His voice, and by holding fast to Him...."* NASB

Time and time again, we see the Israelites being prosperous and victorious over their enemies as they walk with God and trust in Him. God blesses them. He increases their flocks and herds and protects them from disease, blight and sickness. He gives them peace on every side. They are undefeatable as long as they honor God. However, as we read through the Old Testament, we see that time after time the children of Israel choose to go their own way, rebelling against God and worshipping idols. This led to destruction, death and defeat, slavery and oppression, even famine and disease. These things were written as examples for you and me. It was when Israel sinned against God that the people experienced defeat and oppression.

In I Samuel we read about Saul who was anointed king of Israel. The Spirit of the Lord came upon him, and he even prophesied. Saul was even numbered among the prophets (I Samuel 10:11.) God gave Saul position, power, and victory over his enemies as he continually defeated the Philistines. Unfortunately, over time, Saul started to give way to pride and the fear of man. He disobeyed God repeatedly, and this began his descent toward destruction. A man who started with so much promise sadly came to a point where he ended his own life as a defeated and demonically tormented man.

There are many more examples in scripture of people who walked in God's blessing and victory only to lose what they had because of disobedience and the insistence on going their own way. Many believers start their journey with Christ with some degree of wounding, some place of weakness that causes them to struggle with sin or give place to the enemy's lies. Remember, that the children of Israel after crossing the wilderness had to learn to be courageous, fight battles, and win battles before they could enter their Promised Land.

Many Christians today live powerless and defeated lives because they make provisions for sin or come into agreement with the enemy's lies. This gives the enemy grounds to attack and oppress them. Many struggle with their marriage, health, finances, employment or living situation because the enemy has grounds or access to some area in their lives. Like the children of Israel, the believer must learn to walk in holiness, be courageous, and fight the spiritual battles. Each child of God must learn who they are in Christ. We must learn to walk in spiritual authority and power and begin taking ground from the enemy.

Let me illustrate this idea with a word picture. Consider God's protection, provision, and blessing to be an umbrella. The umbrella represents the believer's Promised Land. I consider the believer's Promised Land to be a place of victory. You remain under the umbrella by living a God-honoring life of faith, obedience, and service. This life of faith and obedience in practical terms means embracing your identity and fulfilling God's call and commission as mandated by scripture. (Genesis 1:28, Matthew 28:18-20, Mark 16:15-18.) It means learning to use your authority and take your place as God's representative. It means subduing the earth by destroying the works of the devil. *"The Son of man appeared for this purpose, to destroy the works of the devil."* (1John 3:8) Like the children of Israel, we must enter our Promised Land by first destroying enemy occupation. We must first take the ground in our own lives. Once we have done this, we begin to experience breakthrough and victory in the various other areas of our lives. We begin to learn to walk as Jesus walked.

If you have lived any length of time as a pagan in the secular world you are likely to be opposed by the demonic trying to keep you from remaining under God's umbrella. As you walk in faith, you continue to receive the benefits of God's covering over your life. When you sin, you have the provision of Christ's blood to wash away your sin as you confess and repent of sin. This keeps you under the umbrella. The problem comes when we either believe the enemy's lie that we are not forgiven or continue in a lifestyle and practice of sin. That is why sin must be defeated in our lives if we are to experience the full potential of what God intends for the life of the believer.

THE PASSIVE BELIEVER

Consequently, you cannot enter into the fullness of the Christian life as a passive believer. Moreover, passivity leaves the believer vulnerable to attack. I say this because the implied mandate in all of scripture requires a forward momentum.

(Be fruitful, multiply and subdue the earth ... Genesis 1:28, Go preach...heal the sick, raise the dead, cleanse the lepers, cast out demons... Matthew 10:7-8, Go therefore and make disciples... Matthew 28:19). Our faith is never to be passive. God is always moving, always working, bringing about His intended purpose. God is never static. If we are not moving with Him, we are not walking with Him. Many Christians today live spiritually passive lives, their faith being nothing more than another addition to their otherwise busy lives. This is a dangerous position because the devil is never passive. In 1Peter 5:8 we read, *"Be of sober spirit, be on the alert. Your adversary, the devil prowls around like a roaring lion, seeking someone to devour."* Every night the news media will give you a running commentary on how many unfortunate souls have been devoured by the evil one. Jesus tells us in John 10:10 that *the enemy comes to steal, kill and destroy,* but He also goes on to say that *He (Jesus) came that we might have life and have it more abundantly.* If you understand the tension between those two statements, you will realize that there is no neutral ground. The nominal and complacent believer will never enter into the power and authority that is potentially available to every believer.

God is calling His church to rule and reign with Christ by taking an aggressive posture toward the devil. We are called to destroy the works of the devil by plundering hell and advancing the kingdom of God wherever we go.

VERTICAL AND HORIZONTAL WARFARE

The story I shared at the beginning of this chapter illustrates another general rule I want to cover regarding vertical warfare. Vertical warfare is generally not to be practiced. By vertical warfare I mean praying and speaking directly against demonic principalities and rulers over regions. We are never to do this alone and without having received direction from God. I say this for two reasons. One reason is there is no precedent in scripture for this practice. Jesus didn't even model directly speaking against principalities and other regional forces himself. He certainly had the authority to do so, but He avoided doing so for our benefit. I believe His example does not encourage us in this practice. The only scriptures that show Jesus engaging in vertical warfare are when Jesus rebuked the wind and the waves. However, it appears that He was commanding creation rather than speaking to regional powers (Luke 8:24).

The second reason I do not recommend vertical warfare is because of my firsthand experience with this practice. When I prayed in such a manner, I did so alone and without having received direction from God. This brought the focus of the adversary's attention on me alone. Not a good situation to be in! Instead, I would always recommend corporate prayer led by people who are hearing God and receiving their directives from Him.

There are Christians who practice "Terraforming" (a subject I will address in more detail in chapter 7) who pray against regional spirits, but they never pray alone, and they seek their guidance from the Holy Spirit. I will say more about the subject of Terraforming later on in this book.

When Jesus and the disciples prayed, it was always on the horizontal plane. They would pray for the sick, the diseased, and the demonized. Paul prayed for the church. On the horizontal plane, the disciple has total authority. We as believers have been given authority to tread (horizontally) "over serpents and scorpions and over all the power of the enemy, and nothing shall injure us" (Luke 10:19). It's important to note that both serpents and scorpions (representing demonic types) live close to the ground. These are the "garden variety" type demons. That is to say, they don't rule over regions. Anything bigger should be dealt with in a corporate gathering.

God has given us back what Adam lost. We have been given authority over creation and over all the power the enemy might try to exercise over mankind. Jesus came to destroy the works of the devil. Therefore, our focus must be on demolishing and undoing the works of the adversary. We do this by loving people and by exercising our God-given authority to heal and set free those who were formerly in bondage to the enemy. It's by loving people and bringing redemption to them through salvation, healing, and deliverance that the works of the devil will ultimately be destroyed. Love must be the context out of which we do the works of God. Next, we will look at "love," this most critically important aspect of warfare.

CHAPTER 3

LOVE – OUR MANTLE, OUR MOTIVE

"If I Speak with the tongues of men and of angels, but do not have love, I have become a noisy gong or a clanging cymbal. And if I have the gift of prophecy and can know all mysteries, and have all knowledge: and if I have all faith so as to remove mountains, but do not have love I am nothing. And if I give all my possessions to feed the poor, and I deliver my body to be burned, but do not have love, it profits me nothing."
I Corinthians 13:1-3 NASB

After college I was living in an apartment with three other roommates. Money was tight, and I was working for the YMCA as a day camp counselor at the time. My Volkswagen Bug had just died, and I had discovered after getting it repaired that it was unable to pass the new smog requirements for California. So I had a junk dealer pick it up for $150.00. With that money I bought a bicycle for transportation that I used to make my daily 18 mile trek to and from work.

It was a hot September Friday afternoon in Fullerton, and I had just finished a long week at the Y. I had just come back from a long, hot bike ride when I decided to stop at the Circle K for a cold drink before going home. As I was locking up my bike, I noticed someone who looked like a homeless man staring in my direction. I immediately thought to myself, *"Oh great! He's going to ask me for some money. I'm hot. I'm tired. I don't have much money. And besides, I work hard for my money, and the last thing that I want to do right now is give it away!"* Not very Christ-like I know. When the man approached me, he asked me for some money. I ignored him, and without even answering him I went into the store.

As I went to pour my drink, God said, *"I want you to give him some money."* I said, "Noooo... I haven't got that much!" I spent the next 15 minutes pacing the aisles of Circle K arguing with God about giving this man some money. Finally, for some peace of mind, I just decided to give the man some money. (I know, this was not one of my shining moments').

When I came out, the man approached me and asked, "Can you help me out, sir?" So I took out a few bills and gave them to him. He said, "Thank you." Then I snapped back, "Don't thank me! I wasn't going to give it to you!" Then the man did something I will never forget. He placed his hand on my shoulder, and said, "I'm not called of God, but you are, and God has your heart." Then he started to pray. As he stood there praying for me, the Holy Spirit fell, and I broke down sobbing right there in front of Circle K. With my nose running and my eyes red, I collected myself and went home. Numerous times I passed by that store again looking for the man, but I never saw him again. I have often wondered if he was an angel.

LOVE IS A COMMAND

I share this story with you because love is, first of all, a command of God. Few of us love as much as we could or even the way we should. I'm not proud of the story I just shared with you, but even still, God rewarded me with the touch of His

Spirit for my obedience. I share this because many of us feel that we don't love enough, or even have much love for others to begin with. That's why it's important to know that love is not primarily a feeling. Love, is first of all, a choice. Jesus said, *"A new commandment I give you that you love one another, even as I have loved you, that you also love one another. By this all men will know that you are my disciples, if you have love for one another."* John 13:34-35

This is the most important point I want to stress because love is the most powerful of weapons in your spiritual arsenal. Love is disarming. Love is transformational. Love is the most powerful change agent there is. Love is the one thing that must characterize and contextualize everything we do for Father God. Everything is to be done out of love. Everything is to be framed in love. I shared my story because love almost never starts out as a feeling. Love is a choice. It is a decision of the will. Love is, first of all, an act of obedience.

LOVE IS AN ACTION

Love is an action word. It is something we demonstrate to show that we care. In Gary Chapman's book The *Five Love Languages,* he describes these five ways of experiencing love: *Words of Affirmation, Quality Time, Gift Giving, Acts of Service, and Physical Touch.* It's important to note that all these so-called love languages involve some kind of action, something you do with or for another person.

One time when I was in Bible College my friends secretly planned a surprise birthday party for me. I never saw it coming. The impact it had on me was profound. God used it to bring a healing to my heart and to give me a revelation of His love for me. As I looked around to see all who came to bless me,

I was completely caught off guard and undone. A flood of tears came, and I literally broke down sobbing before I could do anything to compose myself. The action taken by my friends gave an avenue for God's love to literally ambush me! The loving action taken by my friends went completely around all my defenses and intellect and was very humbling. The point is, God's love is often shown through the actions of people.

FILLED WITH GOD'S LOVE

"Beloved, let us love one another, for love is from God; and everyone who loves is born of God and knows God. The one who does not love does not know God, for God is love."

I John 5:7-8

If God is love, and we are filled with God, how can we not love others? Unless, of course, we are not being filled with God.

If God is the source of love, we must be filled with God if we are to love as Jesus loved. The fact is, actions of love often foster feelings of love not only in the person being loved, but also in the person acting in love. I can't tell you how many times that, in the act of praying for someone, I received what I can only describe as a download of God's love and compassion for that person. It can be quite embarrassing at times when tears come to your eyes for someone you don't even know. I've even started the habit of explaining to the person what is happening to give them some understanding. I will say things like, "These tears are coming from God because God wants you to know how much love and compassion He has for you." Or I will say, "God is downloading His heart for you in me, so that you can see how much compassion and mercy He has for you and your situation." It often makes a powerful point to the person being prayed for.

LOVE AND WARFARE

In spiritual warfare, God's love must always be on display, front and center stage. The bottom line is that everything God does reveals His love for mankind. Jesus brought salvation, healing, and deliverance to demonstrate His love. He came to destroy the devil's works because in His love, He desired to set us free. We, as His emissaries, must do the same. In all that we do and say, we must always emphasize God's love for people.

Love is a powerful weapon against darkness. Fear is the adversary's primary weapon in this world. It's love that destroys fear. Fear has dominated the planet ever since sin and death entered through Adam. Jesus came to this earth so that through His single sacrificial act of love on the cross, He would conquer sin and death for us. Sin and death give fear a foothold. Sin and death give fear it's power. By defeating sin and death, Jesus defused fear of its power. He did this through an act of love.

> *"There is no fear in love; but perfect love casts out* (the spirit of) *fear, because fear involves punishment, and the one who fears is not perfected in love."*
> I John 4:18 NASB

It was the perfect love of Christ that defeated sin and death, thus conquering fear by shedding His blood on the cross. It is the *blood* of Christ that we will take a look at in the next chapter.

CHAPTER 4

THE BELIEVER'S SPIRITUAL WEAPONRY

THE BLOOD OF CHRIST

"Much more then, having now been justified by His blood,
we shall be saved from the wrath of God through Him.
For while we were enemies, we were reconciled to God
through the death of His Son, much more, having been
reconciled, we shall be saved by His life. And not only this,
but we also exult in God through our Lord Jesus Christ,
through whom we now receive the reconciliation."
Romans 5:9-11 NASB

There was a time in my life when I was tormented by the demonic. Often my sleep was interrupted by being shaken awake, having bad dreams, or by other demonic manifestations. It was during this season of my life that I was going through my own healing. I was attending Anaheim Vineyard Christian Fellowship and was receiving inner healing prayer ministry from the various ministry teams that were available through the church. It was during this period of time that someone suggested I get into the practice of using oil to plead the blood of Jesus over myself before going to bed. So I would anoint my forehead with oil, pleading the blood of Jesus over myself. This proved to be an invaluable practice for me. It suppressed the manifestations and allowed me to sleep at night while I was getting free from the lies and the pain of my past.

It was during this season that I was attending college. I already mentioned that back in my college days I served as part of the security staff on my campus. One Saturday night as I was out patrolling the campus, a couple of women approached me to report a suspicious man walking around the women's dormitory. When I got to the building, I noticed what looked like a homeless man, somewhat inebriated, standing in front of the women's dorm rooms. As I approached him I noticed that he was heavyset with bulging eyes. I said,

"Hey man, what's going on?" Then he began to stare at me and march in place. As he did so, he began singing the Marine Corps Hymn. *"We will fight this country's battles, the United States Marines....Better watch it, keep covering yourself in the blood."* He made a hand motion across his forehead as he said it. Now I had never met this man in my life. So, I realized at that moment that I was being addressed by a demon that knew me. So I said, *"I know who you are, and you're going to lose."* Then the man staggered back, His eyes glazed over, and then he said, *"My name's buddy, and Satan's in my skin!"* Then he turned away and ran as fast as he could down the street. I never saw the man again.

I share this story with you because it reveals just how threatened the adversary is regarding the blood of Christ. I often refer to my college years mainly because it was a time period when I learned a lot about the practical benefits of spiritual warfare. I was going through my personal deliverance at the time, and my desperation to be free from the demonic taught me to value the various aspects of my faith, not the least of which was the blood of Jesus. Most believers know and understand that Christ's blood pays for their sins and saves them from judgment. (Romans 5:9) But not as many

Christians realize what the ongoing application of Christ's blood can provide. The blood of Jesus provides freedom from condemnation and guilt, seals and protects, preserves, and also cleanses objects and rooms.

THE BLOOD CLEANSES

God in His wisdom often uses natural things to reflect spiritual realities. One example is blood itself. Blood in the human body serves to fight infection and the invasion of foreign bodies. This keeps us from any serious effects of illness. In the same way, the blood of Christ prevents the enemy of our soul from gaining a foothold in our lives. The blood continues to fight the infection of sin. Often, as we go through our workday mixing with the world, we become defiled because of some weakness or failure we have. On other occasions we may feel heaviness in our own spirit (I've heard it described as "being slimed") because of words spoken or the atmosphere in our workplace. It's the blood of Jesus that cleanses us from all defilement. I often feel renewed after applying the blood of Christ to my life. If you have worked hard all day, and you're hot, sweaty and dirty, you would naturally take a shower, right? I feel great after a shower! Pleading the blood of Jesus over yourself is like taking a spiritual shower. I apply the blood of Jesus daily, just as I shower daily.

THE BLOOD PROTECTS AND COVERS

The blood of Christ also serves to protect the believer by acting as a covering. In the book of Exodus, when God is about to bring His last judgment on the Egyptians before delivering

Israel out of bondage, He warns them that He is about to smite the first-born of every family in Egypt by means of a plague. Then He tells the Israelites through His servant Moses that they are to smear a lamb's blood on the doorposts of their homes so the angel of death will pass over. Then, and only then, would that house be protected from God's judgment. Now this obviously is a foreshadowing of Christ's sacrifice, but it supports a fundamental truth regarding the blood of Jesus: it provides protections and covering from spiritual attack if you apply it.

My wife Lori and I serve at a Healing Rooms ministry in our town. Through the years we have made a habit of praying the blood of Christ over ourselves before and after heavy nights of ministry. There have been times when we have failed to do this, and we have paid for it with restless nights of sleeplessness and counterattack. On occasions when we have perceived our sleeplessness as an attack from a demonic source, we have prayed the blood of Jesus over ourselves with the result that we slept like babies for the rest of the night. We have also prayed the blood of Christ over a group that meets at our house on a regular basis. This, I believe, has kept the demonic from interfering with our group discussions. I often pray the blood of Christ over my home and my workplace. Again, I believe this practice provides protection over my house and workplace and serves to suppress demonic activity.

THE BLOOD SEALS AND PRESERVES

The blood of Christ also seals and preserves. After a ministry session, people often receive significant healing or breakthrough. They can also feel somewhat vulnerable when they feel raw with emotion. I have found that sealing with the blood of Christ what God has done in a person helps them keep their healing and preserve what the Holy Spirit has accomplished in them. The healing of memories and past hurts is often a process that can be ongoing for some length of time. So, we want to prevent the adversary from stealing or destroying God's work in a person's life. Applying the blood also helps to preserve physical healing in the event that the enemy attacks someone with lies, trying to get them to question their healing. Applying the blood can help prevent the sabotage of recent ministry.

The blood of Christ is foundational to all ministry and all other spiritual weapons. Everything we have access to as believers we appropriate through the blood. It gives us access to God so that we are able to enter into His presence. The blood allows us to be intimate with God. It enables us to truly worship Him in spirit and in truth, to come before Him with arms raised and His praises on our lips. Worship will be the subject of the next chapter.

CHAPTER 5

WORSHIP

"Praise the Lord! Praise God in His sanctuary; Praise Him in His mighty expanse. Praise Him for His mighty deeds; Praise Him for His excellent greatness. Praise Him with the trumpet sound; Praise Him with the harp and the lyre. Praise Him with the timbrel and dancing; Praise Him with stringed instruments and pipe. Praise Him with loud cymbals. Let everything that has breath praise the Lord. Praise the Lord!"

Psalm 150 NASB

Worship is another huge topic that I will not fully address here. Most importantly, worship is never a means to an end. Worship IS the end! Worship is the end in and of itself. We exist and were created to worship our Father in Heaven. As Jesus said, if we fail to give Him praise, the very rocks will cry out! (Luke 19:40) Again, I will say that worship should never be perceived as "a means to an end," Worship is how we express our love and adoration toward God. Worship is how we pour ourselves out to the Lord, expressing our appreciation of Him. However, worship is also a powerful weapon of spiritual warfare. For our purposes, I will address the subject of worship as it pertains to spiritual warfare. And although worship may take on many forms, I will be referring to worship strictly as musical song and/or the praise of our lips.

I will never forget a time in the early 90's when I was at church on a Sunday evening and Kevin Prosh was leading worship. As the worship progressed that evening, the Spirit of God invaded the sanctuary. It was as if the Father had arrived just to play with His children. I could only describe it as an atmosphere of extreme joy and celebration. Young people began dancing and running clockwise around a very large sanctuary and jumping off the stage where Kevin and the band were playing. People were being touched by the Holy Spirit. Tears flowed, laughter broke out, and people were healed and set free. It seemed for a brief moment that Heaven had actually come down to earth, and every care was forgotten, if only for that moment.

Worship evokes the presence of God, and with His presence come all the blessings of the kingdom such as salvation, healing, deliverance, or spiritual gifts. Every significant movement in church history took place because a group of God's people decided to get together to pray, worship, and passionately seek Him. It is a powerful thing when God's people passionately seek Him in worship. When God's people worship, Hell is shaken. When God shows up, Hell is pillaged.

BATTLES ARE WON THROUGH WORSHIP

Battles are won beginning with worship. In 2 Chronicles 20 King Jehoshaphat and Judah are threatened by the sons of Ammon and Moab (a vastly superior army.) Then some of the king's men came to Jehoshaphat saying great multitudes are coming against you from beyond the sea! Jehoshaphat was afraid, so he turned his attention to seek the Lord and proclaimed a fast for all of Judah. As Judah corporately sought the Lord, in the midst of the assembly the Spirit of the Lord came upon Jahaziel, the son of Zechariah. Then the Lord spoke through Jahaziel and said, *"You need not fight in this battle; station yourselves and see the salvation of the Lord. Do not fear or be dismayed; for the Lord is with you. Tomorrow, go out and face them for the Lord is with you"* (II Chronicles 20:15-16 NASB).

The next day King Jehoshaphat appointed those who sang to the Lord and those who praised Him. When Judah began singing and praising the God of Heaven, the Lord set ambushes against the sons of Ammon. A battle broke out between Ammon and the forces allied with them so that in the confusion they began to destroy one another. Later when the forces of Judah looked out toward the wilderness, they saw nothing but corpses lying on the ground and no one had escaped. It was through Judah's worship that God released the ambushes against the enemies of God's people.

So it is true today. Worship releases the power of God that brings Heaven's resources to bear on the darkest of situations. You may be feeling overwhelmed by some big challenges. Maybe you've experienced a job loss, or maybe you're going through some major financial loss. Begin to worship God. Maybe your marriage is under attack, and the more you try to fix it, the worse it gets. Begin worshipping God. Maybe your business is going under, or you've just received the worst case scenario from your physician. Worship the Lord with all your strength! What will happen is God will begin getting bigger, and your problem will start to shrink.

WORSHIP DISPELS DARKNESS

It's been said that if you want to dispel darkness, turn on the light. Remember, our battle is not against flesh and blood. Our enemies are spirits of darkness. Although worship is not a means to any end but glorifying God, one of the most glorious things about worshipping our God is that it evokes His presence. It's the manifestation of God's presence that dispels spiritual darkness. I will often suggest to people who are in the process of healing and deliverance to play worship very low in their bedrooms at night all night. I did this when I was going through my deliverance, and it diminished demonic manifestations and stayed the enemy's hand, allowing me to sleep. Christian worship is a powerful deterrent of the demonic and often repels the presence of evil. CD's or IPODS with worship songs played continuously on a loop work perfectly for this. In the darkest periods of my life when the enemy was pressing down on me, and I felt the most alone and even despaired, fearing the worst would come, worship brought the needed breakthrough.

WORSHIP BRINGS BREAKTHROUGH

I have found that personal worship brings breakthrough in prayer and in my personal time with God. Many times it is worship that ushers in God's manifest presence and fills me with His peace and His power. Anointing often comes during worship as we minister to the Lord our appreciation and love for Him. It is the presence of God that brings breakthrough in revelation, healing, and deliverance.

If you are feeling dry and apathetic in your relationship with God, I would encourage you to set aside time to press into

God in worship. God will not delay long in meeting with you. If there are obstacles or something is blocking your intimacy with the Lord, He will reveal it in worship. It's worship that clears the spiritual fog that sometimes clouds our minds.

Oftentimes we can feel overwhelmed with life's responsibilities and distractions. Sometimes we feel squeezed by time constraints and the many tasks on our "To Do" lists. I have found the greatest breakthroughs have come in worship. Worship magnifies the Lord and puts all other things in perspective. It is in the place of worship that we find our sanctuary and our place of rest. We are refreshed. We are again reminded that God is with us, God is on our side, God loves us, and He is for us and not against us. God is strong on our behalf. He will defend, preserve, strengthen, and establish us. God is faithful, and He will uphold us with His righteous right arm. (Isaiah 41:10)

> *"Come, let us worship and bow down, let us kneel before the Lord our Maker. For He is our God, and we are the people of His pasture, and the sheep of His hand."*
>
> Psalm 95:6-7

CHAPTER 6

FORGIVENESS

"Jesus said to them again, 'Peace be with you; as the Father has sent Me, I also send you.' And when He had said this, He breathed on them and said to them, 'Receive the Holy Spirit. If you forgive the sins of any, their sins have been forgiven them; if you retain the sins of any, they have been retained."
John 20:21-23 NASB

Andy (not his real name) had come for prayer once a week for several weeks without any visible breakthrough. He seemed emotionless and very controlled in his expression and demeanor. Over the course of the next few weeks we began to hear more of Andy's story.

Andy was raised in a hyper-critical and verbally abusive family; His father and mother were very demeaning and belittling to him. Throughout his life his parents were extremely harsh in their words regarding anything Andy said or did. He was constantly derided for his grades, his friends, his interests. As he became an adult, Andy became increasingly angry. This anger was very controlled, but was always just beneath the surface. Because Andy was never allowed to have an opinion, he was also kept from expressing any of his own feelings. Never having been validated, Andy was unable to express his emotions. Years later, when he asked my wife Lori and me for prayer, he was bitter and withdrawn which kept him closed off from others and made relationships difficult.

Andy knew he needed help, and so he came asking for prayer. As he began to share his story, I could tell that he was intelligent and articulate. After sharing, it became obvious that he was going to need to forgive his parents. As we led him through a prayer to forgive and release his parents, the Holy Spirit showed me that Andy needed to be released from shame. (Shame is self-rejection.) As the Holy Spirit ministered, Andy began to experience a slight release of emotion as he forgave himself. Tears came ever so slightly. Breakthrough! Then the Holy Spirit directed me to tell Andy to do something. I said, "Andy, God wants you to shout 'I'm free!' at the top of your lungs." He struggled to say it and felt self-conscious about being loud, but in the end he shouted, "I'm free!" There was visible release as a smile came to his face. By the time Andy left, his countenance had changed, and His joy was evident.

Believing the enemy's lie, Andy had been bound and had remained emotionally and relationally crippled much of his life. Believing lies is agreement with the adversary. Mankind fell in the garden because Adam and Eve believed the lie spun by Lucifer. When they accepted the lie, they agreed to the sin. This brought in shame and fear. That is why Adam and Eve hid themselves from the Lord when he came looking for them. Whenever we believe the enemy, we are coming into agreement with him. When we come into agreement with the devil, we empower him. The devil gains power over our lives through agreement. For the believer, this agreement often comes in the form of judgment and self-condemnation.

Unforgiveness is harboring judgment against ourselves or others. It is holding condemnation over ourselves or others. God's word says in Romans 8:1, *"There is therefore now no* condemnation for those who are in Christ Jesus." Our unforgiveness of ourselves or others is agreement with the enemy. Unforgiveness gives the devil a foothold and a doorway of influence in our lives. Unforgiveness gives the enemy grounds to torment us. This is why we are encouraged in scriptures "... *Do not let the sun go down on your anger, and do not give the devil an opportunity"* (Ephesians 4:26). Unforgiveness leads to bitterness which, over time, can cause all kinds of psychological and even physical maladies. Unforgiveness keeps us under judgment and condemnation. Jesus said in Matthew 6:14-15, *"For if you forgive others for their transgressions, your heavenly Father will also forgive you. But if you do not forgive others, then your Father will not forgive your transgressions."*

Now, here's how forgiveness works as a spiritual weapon to help us plunder the kingdom of darkness. As Christ's body, we have been given the keys of the kingdom (Matt. 16: 19). Jesus said, *If you forgive the sins of any, their sins have been forgiven them; if you retain the sins of any, they have been retained"* (John 20:23). Jesus said that whatever we bind on earth will have been bound in heaven, and whatever we loose on earth will have been loosed in heaven (Matt. 16:19). This is a profound and empowering statement for believers.

If unforgiveness empowers Satan and allows him to gain influence and control, what happens when we as the church extend forgiveness? We cut off the enemy's legs right out from under him! We take away his grounds and his rights to exert influence.

When we as the church hold judgment over cities and regions known for being seedbeds of sin, cities like New York, Chicago, Las Vegas, and San Francisco, we retain the sins of those cities against them, thus empowering the enemy to exercise his influence on them. Could it be that these cities have remained quagmires of sin and debauchery because of Christians' judgments against them? As representatives of Jesus Christ, are we not called to walk as Jesus walked? God so loved the world that he extended forgiveness of sin to the world by sending his own Son to die on a cross (John 3:16). Jesus prayed while dying on that cross, *"Father forgive them, for they know not what they do"* (Luke 23:34, NASB). What if we, as the church, with the same heart as our Lord, began to forgive and remit the sins of these great cities? Perhaps it would allow God to move in these cities with greater influence. Is it possible that judgments and sins retained by the churches, are keeping revival from breaking out in some of the darkest places in our world?

To forgive and remit the sins of these cities may, in fact, allow God's Holy Spirit to move in these places with great effect, thus giving the church more freedom and success in reaching the lost, healing the sick, and delivering the demonized. Moreover, it could even have an impact on municipal laws and political policies that do not consider godly values. (The implications of this are profound!) Think about a city whose sins have been covered in the blood of Christ and whose sins have been forgiven by the church. Think about a city where the devil no longer has any grounds or rights to influence or occupy. Think about a city where there is little or no supernatural opposition to the church! Imagine what God could do under those circumstances!

It is a powerful and awesome position of authority and responsibility to pronounce forgiveness over people. I have on occasion laid hands on people, pronouncing them forgiven, with incredible results in breakthrough and release for the person. Forgiveness is a powerful spiritual weapon and is another well-kept secret in Christianity.

As a general practice, I pray a covering over my workplace before starting in the morning. Parts of my prayers involve praying forgiveness over my workplace and my coworkers. Praying this way allows the Spirit of God to move on behalf of my coworkers, binding the spirits of lies, gossip, dissensions, factions and strife. This is a critical step to cleansing the atmosphere in my work environment. It takes away any demonic foothold that the enemy could use to create havoc or hostility in my workplace. With no sin for the enemy to latch onto, he is rendered powerless. We as sons and daughters of the King of all kings have the authority to not only forgive sins, but also the authority to bind the strongman. *"Or how can anyone enter the strong man's house and carry off his property, unless he first binds the strong man? And then he will plunder his house." Matthew 12:29*

Forgiveness is one of the primary means of removing the devil's rights to a person or place. This is what has come to be known as "Terraforming," and is the next spiritual weapon I want to address.

CHAPTER 7

TERRAFORMING

"...for the weapons of our warfare are not of the flesh, but divinely powerful for the destruction of fortresses. We are destroying speculations and every lofty thing raised up against the knowledge of God, and we are taking every thought captive to the obedience of Christ..."
2 Corinthians 10:4 NASB

The term "Terraforming" is used by Scott J. Norval in his book *Terraforming for the Kingdom* and is borrowed from science fiction for its close parallels to spiritual warfare.

Terraforming: To alter the atmosphere of a planet previously harsh and antagonistic to life, thereby making it livable and life-supporting.

I started working as a security officer at the courthouse in 2006. I have worked for eight years at the local courthouse in our town. Our job as security is to insure the safety of all government and public personnel. We do this by screening people who come into the courthouse to make sure that they have no weapons or contraband. There are only two public entrances into the building consisting of three metal detection gates, two on the north side and one on the south. Each gate is manned by two guards and we are usually paired up with a different person each week. We often work ten hour days which gives us a lot of time to talk and think when we are not in the midst of the morning or lunchtime rush. When I started working there, I noticed a couple of things right away. First of all, I noticed how political the workplace culture was. Any conversation involving "the big four" (politics, religion, sex and race) was automatically off limits. This is not unusual for any place of employment. However, when you are a zealous Christian like I am, and you are working with someone for ten hours a day, the subject of faith is bound to come up now and then, especially when your Christianity is so much a part of who you are, like it is with me.

The second thing I noticed was how territorial the guards were about their jobs. Officers who had been there longer than I were quick to let me know about that. Consequently, there was a distinct pecking order, a fine line as to who was "in" and who was "out." This basically meant that if you crossed, looked sideways at, or disagreed with those who were "in", you could find yourself out of that duty station and stuck on some "ghost post." This is where they would often put the screw-ups, dissenters and the politically incorrect.

The third thing I noticed about the environment in my workplace was how hyper-sensitive my co-workers and much of the public seemed to be. People would take offense at how rules were enforced, or at a look, or at a tone of voice. They would even take offense at subject matter in a conversation that they weren't even involved in! For example, on numerous occasions public personnel would come through the gate of the courthouse and interpret the look or the tone of a particular officer as offensive. Now those looks or tones may truly occur from time to time, but that does not seem unusual in a public place with a high volume of people coming through.

However, what I did find unusual was how complaints that were relatively minor, and should have been easily resolved, ended up ballooning into bigger issues from management to supervisor. Write-ups and written reprimands soon followed. It was at this point that I suspected that something demonic and unseen was going on in my workplace. There were many instances of this nature, people getting upset over relatively minor, insignificant things. Moreover, it was cultivating an atmosphere of fear and paralysis in the workplace. I felt myself being forced to conform to a mold. I was slowly becoming a drone, a deadpan, emotionless robot. This, in turn, created a very sterile and boring work environment. It began to zap the joy out of my co-workers, and I could see it.

Another example of this hyper-sensitivity was seen in anonymous reports given to supervisors. I found it very strange that in the middle of a conversation with a coworker about personal matters of the heart or issues of faith, I would be called downstairs and given a written reprimand regarding a complaint by an anonymous third party. These individuals never confronted or spoke to me personally, and they never would identify themselves, so I was never afforded the opportunity to confront my accusers. Now, I know what some of you are thinking, YOU SHOULDN'T BE TALKING ABOUT YOUR FAITH AT WORK! I'm not arguing that point. What I am doing is asking these questions: Is there more going on that has brought about these rules common to many places of employment? Is there something spiritually sinister promoting this kind of environment? Is our adversary actively seeking to sterilize our work environment against our faith? Is there a demonic influence not only constructing these rules, but more importantly, enforcing them by creating this hyper-sensitivity in the workplace?

And if so, what can we do about it? These are the questions I began to ask myself.

I intuitively knew there was a bully in my workplace, and I knew that the bully was demonic and spiritual in nature, but what could I do about it?

Then I remembered the scripture when Jesus said; *"Or how can anyone enter the strong man's house and carry off his property, unless he first binds the strong man? And then he will plunder his house." Matthew 12:29* NASB

I began to do some study and some investigation into spiritual warfare seeking answers to what might be done about this intimidating bully. It wasn't long after this that I heard about a "Terraforming" seminar being held at one of the local churches in my area, so I decided to check it out. Now you're probably wondering the same thing that I was wondering at the time. What in the world is Terraforming? I knew it had something to do with spiritual warfare, so I decided to go and hear what they had to say. Well, as it turns out, the word "Terraforming" was a term actually borrowed from science fiction and is by definition *the act of transforming a hostile environment (or planet) into one that is able to sustain human life.* The spiritual corollary is that we, as royal priests, sons and daughters and representatives of the kingdom of heaven, have been given the authority and the responsibility to make this planet (now made hostile toward humans by demonic spirits) habitable by changing the spiritually hostile atmosphere to one that is life giving. Put another way, we as followers of Jesus are called to displace the kingdom of darkness with the kingdom of light by destroying the works of the devil.

As I sat through the Terraforming conference listening, the speaker talked about praying together as a group and seeking God's directives to bring down territorial spirits over cities and geographical regions. I was intrigued, but leery, having had such negative experiences in my past doing similar things. I knew this kind of prayer got results, but I wanted to be cautious.

As I continued listening, I noticed a few strategies that were different from the way I had previously attempted to do this. The first thing I noticed was that they were in a group, whereas I had been praying alone. The second thing I noticed was that they sought specific guidance and direction from the Holy Spirit as to how He wanted them to pray.

This was different from praying my own "good ideas." The third thing I noticed was that they prayed to God as opposed to speaking against these regional principalities and powers directly. The one thing that was actually similar to what I had been doing was that they, too, would go to the location being prayed over. I began to realize that there might be more to this method of spiritual warfare than I had understood at the time.

CHANGING ATMOSPHERES

Simply put, Terraforming, as I understand it, is displacing the kingdom of darkness in its various forms by bringing the light or the kingdom of God into a situation. The kingdom of God by definition is the rule and reign of Christ. We as God's representatives have been commissioned and given authority to impose the kingdom of God over the kingdom of darkness. We do this by bringing the rule and reign of Christ wherever we go. We do this by walking in spiritual authority and exercising that authority over the places the devil currently occupies.

Here's how it works. I will use my workplace as an example: The devil had authority over my workplace. He had that authority because he had been given grounds and the right to be there and to do what he does. He was given those rights and dominion over my workplace because of the sin of every employee, Christian and non-Christian alike. He was also given rights because of past sins. So the devil and his minions had the right to stir up gossip and bad feelings. He had grounds to create dissensions, factions, and strife among my coworkers. He had grounds to bring complaints and bad reports to management. Moreover, being completely unopposed, he had the freedom to lie and act out his malevolent agenda in my workplace.

Now I, as a son and a royal priest of the kingdom, have been given the keys of the kingdom. If I forgive the sins of any, their sin is forgiven. If I retain the sins of any, their sins are retained (John 20:23). Now we know that there is no forgiveness without the shedding of blood, and we also know that Jesus died for the sins of the world by shedding His blood on the cross. What that means is this – please stay with me – we've been given authority to forgive sins! Do you realize what this means?!!

GOD HAS GIVEN US THE AUTHORITY AND THE MEANS TO TAKE THE DEVIL'S RIGHTS AWAY FROM HIM!

The ramifications of this truth are profound and can impact our lives in very practical ways! We can remit the sins of the people in our workplace for a day, whether they are repentant or not. Hence, this kind of prayer needs to be done daily or the enemy soon regains his rights to act out again since unrepentant people will continue to sin. Without the rights or the grounds to act, the demons must bow to the name of Jesus. Terraforming empowers believers to take dominion over the atmosphere in public places.

So, all the believer has to do is plead the blood of Jesus over their workplace, coworkers, household, family, business or employees, etc., etc., and pronounce them forgiven! Now the believer can exercise his or her God given authority by binding the enemy and telling the devil's minions what they will no longer be allowed to do. This is exactly what I did. I began getting up early in the morning so I could get a cup of coffee, sit in my jeep, and literally pray (out loud) over my family and my workplace. Soon, I began to see signs of immediate change and breakthrough.

As I began learning how to pray effectively to limit demonic activity in my workplace, I immediately began to notice changes in my working environment. For example, I started noticing how much less often people were offended by each other. Schisms, angry feelings and gossip all but died out and were replaced by harmonious and amiable working relationships. Now I am not saying that everything has been perfect and hunky-dory all the time. My coworkers still have arguments and differences from time to time, but now their differences are much less incendiary in nature. Instead of an argument escalating, it simply dies out. People move on and forget their differences. Coworkers complain less to our supervisors. The resolutions to conflicts are more immediate. The public virtually has stopped filing complaints altogether.

I also began to experience more freedom to share my faith in the workplace. I was no longer getting called on the carpet because of the anonymous "third party" overhearing me discussing spiritual matters with a coworker. Oversensitivity of people in general has been replaced by more patience and understanding. A regular and healthy exchange of ideas with my co-workers was now possible without interference, frivolous complaints or the fear of retaliation from demonic sources gaining access to people around us. This experience began to open my eyes to just how much influence these unseen forces have in our day-to-day lives and how we can begin defeating them!

What I began to realize is that much of what we just accept in our daily lives as "normal" has actually been shaped and directed by the enemy of our souls. People commonly say, *"Don't ever talk about your faith at work."* This common constraint is enforced by the demonic realm which creates a hyper-sensitive work environment. This subtle change in our culture over time has now become accepted as "normal." Just so I'm clear, I am *not* talking about a healthy and normal sensitivity to real insult and injury. I am talking about an oversensitivity that is fed and increased exponentially by demonic lies. Demons use this dynamic to foster frivolous complaints. Now the devil has just determined what can and cannot be discussed in the course of regular dialogue. Reasonable freedoms are compromised or lost altogether.

Terraforming is an important spiritual weapon because it cleanses a person, place, or thing and removes the enemy's rights so the believer can exercise their God-given authority to bind and remove demonic influences and strongholds.

Now I will share what I do when I seek to terraform a person, place, or thing. Terraforming happens over a person, place, or thing when they are prayed over. I never start Terraforming until I have first asked the Father for my own forgiveness and cleansing. It is only by the blood of Jesus that we can stand before Him, and I don't want the enemy to have any grounds for retaliation that he can exploit in my life. That is why if you are to begin Terraforming, you must be a seeker of God and embrace holy living.

Terraforming is asking God to cleanse a desired person, place or object. I do this by first asking God to bring His presence to shine through the person, place or object I'm praying for. It is the presence of God that exposes all defilement in a person, place or object causing it to surface. Then I plead the blood of Jesus over whoever or whatever it is that I am seeking to Terraform. Once I have done this, I will ask Father to forgive and remit all sins committed, past and present. Then I ask God to cleanse, wash and purge every person, place, or thing that I am seeking to Terraform. Once this is done, the enemy no longer has any rights to occupy the territory or act out his agenda. It is then I will begin binding and banishing all demonic action and assignments, dissensions, devices, divisions, conspiracies, curses, gossip, bad reports, negative talk, strife, witchcraft and rebellion, pride and arrogance along with all lust. Then I break the power of all lies, spiritual strongholds and fortresses in the mind, soul and body.

Once this is done, I begin to petition the Lord for a prescribed (pray about the number) number of His warring angels to rout any and all enemy occupation in that place. This removes any residual occupation of darkness. Then I ask for the angels to stand watch and guard the person, place or thing. This has proven to be very effective in my workplace, and is an invaluable tool for any believer in spiritual warfare. However, I want to stress that this should be done every day, especially when praying over unbelievers or the unrepentant.

It is through the process of Terraforming that we can successfully remove the enemy's influence in our marriages, families, homes, workplaces, ministries, churches, schools or government. Any of these areas can be Terraformed if we are willing to give them the time and attention.

I have even Terraformed my own family to keep the enemy from interfering in our relationships. My wife and I have two children, and kids can argue from time to time. Anyone with young kids knows how true this is. The problem is that kids of a tender age can become vulnerable to demonic influence without proper prayer cover. As the man of the house I understood it was my responsibility to cover my marriage and my family with prayer. Prior to my knowledge of Terraforming, when our kids argued, the arguments would often escalate into more incendiary and mean-spirited verbal attacks, very uncharacteristic of how we have raised them. Now I know what some of you are thinking. *"Kids will be kids."* However, my sensitivity to God and spiritual things told me there was more going on than just regular conflict between siblings. Something about the level of intensity and malice that ensued told me there was much more going on, something demonic. The enemy was attempting to heat things up to hurt, wound, and destroy the relationship between brother and sister.

When I started Terraforming my household, I would jump into my jeep and drive to a lonely spot where I like to pray and have my devotions in the morning. It was there that I began to Terraform by lifting up my family in prayer. I would pray for covering and protection over my home, my marriage, and over my kids. I would do this by thanking God for my family and all the things He has blessed me with. Then I would plead the blood of Jesus over myself and my family members individually. I would then plead the blood over our home and property, asking God to forgive us our sins. Once this was done, I would pray the full armor of God (Ephesians 6) over all of us. I would also call in angels to rout the enemy and keep Him at bay.

When I began asking God to cover my family, I began to see an immediate difference in the behavior of my children. It's not that they didn't argue. They did. It's not that they were suddenly perfect. They weren't. But in some very subtle ways, and not so subtle ways, they were different. They were communicating more and arguing less. When they did argue, their comments were more constructive and not so hateful and mean. They generally seemed more reasonable overall.

Remember, this approach to spiritual warfare had started out as an experiment based on what I had learned at the Terraforming seminar. Now I have been Terraforming for years in all my different spheres of influence. Now I know that this works, and I am convinced of just how much influence we have as believers over our environment and the world around us. My hope is that you will truly realize that God had given us as Christians the authority to change atmospheres. I want to encourage you to begin exercising this authority in your own circles of influence to become a change agent of God in our world. To help you with this, here is a tool to guide you through the process.

Here is a simple outline to help you remember and follow when you are wanting to Terraform a person or place.

<u>TERRAFORMING OUTLINE</u>

1. First, ask God for your own forgiveness and cleansing.
2. Ask God to shine the light of His presence in, around and through a person, place or object and to expose all things that defile and corrupt.

3. Plead the blood of Jesus, asking God to cleanse, wash and purge the person, place or thing of all defilement and contaminants that came as a result of past sins.
4. Ask God to forgive and remit all sins committed past or present resulting in this defilement.
5. Take authority and remove all rights of the evil one to torment, afflict and intimidate. Render powerless, null, and void all curses, devices, traps and conspiracies and witchcraft.
6. Call in angels to rout any remaining remnant of evil and to stand guard over that person, place or object.
7. Finally, invite God's presence into the person, place or object. Ask Him to dwell there. Give God glory and Honor!

It is by doing this and by making it a practice that you take away the rights of the evil one to occupy and have influence. I have only known about Terraforming for a few years, but it's had such a powerful impact on my family and workplace, that I have a sincere conviction that it is absolutely essential for every believer to know about. For a more comprehensive teaching on terraforming I would highly recommend Scott J. Norvel's book, *Terraforming for The Kingdom*. It is very practical and informative.

Terraforming is implemented through the exercise of our spiritual authority. Spiritual authority is also exercised through our declaration and decree of God's promises and what He has done on our behalf. This is the word of our testimony.

CHAPTER 8

PROPHETIC WEAPONRY & DECLARATION

"For the testimony of Jesus is the spirit of prophecy."
Revelation 19:10

*"And they overcame him by the blood of the Lamb
and because of the word of their testimony..."*
Revelation 12:11 NASB

Some time ago I was in a season of pressing in to hear God. Wanting to hear God, I kept asking Him to use me in the prophetic. "Speak to me, God, so that I can speak to others! Use me, God, so that I can speak into the hearts of others! Give me words, and I will speak them out!" I went on and on like this for quite some time without hearing from God, at least in the time frame that I was anticipating. You know what they say: be careful what you pray for because you just might get it.

Well, some time had passed, and I was at a gas station that had a large automated carwash because my car was so dirty crops could grow on it. So, I left my car with the attendant for a cleaning and decided to wait outside to watch my car come through. As I was sitting on the bench waiting, I noticed a fireman in uniform standing in front of me off to the side, waiting for his car. Then the Lord spoke to me, *"Tell that man that I see his situation, and that everything is going to be ok."* Then I started to think and analyze (something you should never do if you want to operate in prophetic ministry). *Is that God, or is that just me?* Then He spoke a second time, *"Go tell that man that I see his situation, and that everything is going to be ok."* Now I'm going bonkers, thinking, *What if I'm wrong? He's going to think I'm a nut-case! He's going to think that I've got a screw loose.* I sat there reasoning with myself, but the message would not go away. It just kept gnawing at me. Then I thought: *"Well, I have been asking God to speak to me, and now that He is, I can't just ignore it; I need to be obedient. I need to do what God's telling me."* So with a new resolve I stood up and walked over to the fireman. When I approached him, he turned and looked at me to see who I was. Our eyes met and I said, "Sir, I don't normally do this, but God just spoke to me, and He wants you to know that He sees your situation, and that everything is going to be ok."

That was all I said, and the impact on this man was immediately visible. His jaw dropped and tears came to his eyes. My car was ready, so I took the keys from the attendant, jumped in, and drove away. But as I drove away, I glanced over at the fireman. He just stared, his eyes following me as I drove off. I never knew what those words meant to him, but I had the most exciting and fulfilling experience after leaving that carwash!

WORDS OF KNOWLEDGE

The spiritual gift that I was operating out of is called "word of knowledge," which is supernatural revelation or knowledge about a person that you could not know by natural means. It's all part of the full package of what I call "prophetic weaponry." This would include words of knowledge, words of command, fore telling and forth telling, as well as, declaration and decree. It is important to recognize that the first century church was in fact a prophetic movement. By that I mean, they operated and functioned regularly in the prophetic gifts, literally devastating the kingdom of darkness wherever they went. In the first century, disciples operated and functioned with the expectation that they would hear from God. The early church was birthed a prophetic movement (Acts 2:17-18) which allowed it to release miracles, healings, signs and wonders. This was in fulfillment of Joel 2:28-32. This is, in fact, the way God has intended His church to operate, even in the present day. Hearing God enabled Christian believers to be God-directed in their mission. Hearing God is what separates the church from every other mere institution. It is in revelation and prophecy that God lets us in on what He is about to do. That is when the life of the believer gets really exciting!

One time I was praying for a man with a torn meniscus. His knee was bandaged, and he was only able to walk with extreme difficulty. As he eased himself down on the chair for prayer, I began to ask God how He wanted me to pray for him. After waiting on the Lord for a minute or two, God said to me, *"Tell him to jump up."* I began to rub my forehead, as I thought, *"Jump up? You want me to tell someone with a torn meniscus to jump up?!!"* I began to rub my forehead again. The guy watching me looked at me like, "What's up?" So, I just told him. "God told me that he wants you to jump up." The man immediately got up and started to jump around the room, and as he did he was instantly healed. He began yelling, "I'm healed! I'm healed!" The word that I had received from the Lord had released faith in the man, and when he responded in obedience to the word,

God released the miracle. God is awesome! But how he will stretch our faith sometimes!

A word of knowledge is a powerful weapon against the enemy because as God's son or daughter, He is giving you the privilege of inside information regarding what He is about to do. More than that, our Father is allowing us to participate in His ministry. There is nothing like it. You may not even be experiencing much anointing or power, but if God gives you a word of knowledge, it's as good as gold! You can be sure that He will back it up.

WORD OF COMMMAND

A word of command is similar to a gift of faith. It is a "download" from God whereby a powerful and effective prayer of command is given through the believer to the demon, disease or condition resulting in the immediate release of the person from bondage, affliction, sickness or malady. Jesus appeared to use word of command frequently throughout His earthly ministry. One example is when He rebuked a very high fever that was afflicting Peter's mother-in-law (Luke 4:38) *"...Standing over her, He rebuked the fever, and it left her; and she immediately rose and waited on them."*

We also see that Jesus used a word of command when the disciples found their boat getting overwhelmed by a storm (Mark 4:37-39). The passage goes on to say, *"And He got up and rebuked the wind and the waves and said, 'Peace, be still', and the wind died down and it became perfectly calm. 'And He said why are you afraid? Do you still have no faith?"* Early in His ministry, Jesus uses word of command when confronted by a demonized man on the Sabbath in the synagogue. (Mark 1:23-27) Then the demon cries out saying, *"What do we have to do with You Jesus of Nazareth? Have You come to destroy us? I know who You are- the Holy One of God!" And Jesus rebuked him saying, 'Be quiet and come out of him.' And throwing him into convulsions, the unclean spirit cried out with a loud voice, and came out of him. And they were all amazed..."* We see from these passages and others that word of command can be a very effective weapon of spiritual warfare when combined with faith for the moment. One time I was walking in a park on my lunch break when I came across this woman in a wheelchair. As I began talking to her, I learned that she had been limited to the wheelchair because of a severe condition of Lupus, and that she had been in this condition several years. She was so limited by the disease that she was unable to do the most routine tasks without being completely overcome by exhaustion. Earlier, I had heard a testimony from a pastor that Lupus was also known as Wolf's disease, and that he had brought about a successful healing by commanding the Wolf spirit to leave. He said something like, "You filthy, stinking dog,- leave!" Moreover, He also said that he literally saw that spirit slink away like a dog. So, I was feeling a lot of faith and decided to try it. I asked if I could pray for her and she said, yes. I then laid my hand on her shoulder and began to ask the Holy Spirit to release His healing touch. As I started to pray, I began to feel power surging through my hand. (Not something I feel that often) This by itself increased my faith dramatically. I asked God for more power. The surges increased. Then I spoke to the spirit of Lupus and said, "You filthy, stinking dog,-leave her in Jesus name!" I repeated myself again with that same prayer. I continued praying for her until I sensed God was finished. Then after saying goodbye, I left. The following week I was walking around that same park, and I saw that same woman across the street, standing (without her wheelchair) in front of her house watering her grass. She exuberantly waved to me and said hi. She was beaming and appeared to be in very good spirits. The word of command, given in faith, can be a very effective weapon of spiritual warfare when faced with an affliction of demonic origin. Word of command is distinctive and different from declaration or decrees in that its origin comes from a directive or inspiration of the Holy Spirit.

FORE TELLING AND FORTH TELLING

"Life and death are in the power of the tongue,
and those who love it will eat of its fruit
"Proverbs 18:21 NASB

As weapons of spiritual warfare go, when people think of prophecy or the prophetic in general, most people think of "fore telling." That is, someone speaking over a person regarding future events. In fore telling the person giving the prophecy is actually receiving information from God regarding some future calling, direction, circumstance or event. This is for the purpose of encouragement and sometimes confirmation. Fore telling is an important aspect of the prophetic, but not the one we will focus on right now.

One aspect of prophecy that I have found to be interesting, providing breakthrough in my own life, is "forth telling." In fore telling God gives you revelation of future events. In forth telling the believer is making a prophetic declaration or decree into a situation or circumstance by virtue of their spiritual authority or position in Christ. It is the practice of forth telling as a spiritual weapon that I want us to explore in this chapter.

As believers in Christ, God has given us special privilege and position in the spirit realms. As sons and daughters of the King of all kings, many Christians carry more spiritual authority then they will ever know or even realize. This is unfortunate and explains why the impact of the Westernized church remains only marginal. Many believers do not understand the spiritual authority that they carry. It is this authority that gives us the power to change atmospheres and circumstances, even the power to impact our physical reality.

One example of this truth happened some time ago. I often take what I call prayer walks around my neighborhood. It helps me think and gives me a chance to commune with God. On this particular occasion, I was in a season where I was experiencing a lot of faith and anointing. Ministry seemed to be effective, and God was doing a lot of very cool things. Well, as I was walking down this street, I came by an abortion clinic. The very sight of that clinic evoked an anger in my spirit as I thought of all the lives being taken by this institution, so I stopped in front of the clinic, pointed my finger at the building and said out loud, "In Jesus name, I curse the plumbing in this building!" Then I continued to finish my walk. I knew that as a Christian, we should never ever curse people created in the image of God. This was never a consideration in my mind. However, I thought cursing an inanimate object like water pipes would be fair game. After all, Jesus cursed the fig tree, right? It was the very next week that I drove by that abortion clinic and realized that all the landscape in front of the building was completely dug up. I slowed my car and saw that their water pipes were exposed with mounds of dirt piled up on the sides of each trench. Construction horses with blinking lights had been set up to keep passersby away. I continued to drive away amazed that my words actually made an impact on the physical reality, the plumbing in that building.

I share this story to illustrate something that is innate in every believer. This is a positional authority given to every believer as a child of God. This authority actually gives us the ability to prophesy into our own future. Even in circles of psychology, psychologists will talk about the "self-fulfilling prophecy." Why? Because it is recognized (even in secular circles) that our words have the power to change and direct the course of our lives. As believers, that authority is increased exponentially with our spiritual position and anointing. Why? It is because we are sons and daughters of the King. And as such, we've been given authority to rule over the spirit realm, and it's the spirit realm that impacts and shapes the physical reality.

However, before I get ahead of myself, I want to make it clear that our gifts and authority are only to be used for God's purposes. The scriptures tell us that *"God's gifts and His calling are irrevocable"* (Romans 11:29). This means that we can still operate in the gifts of God without necessarily being under His blessing. God's gifts can be abused and manipulated for our own ends. This is something that the Christian may be tempted to do but should avoid in all circumstances. It is the abuse and manipulation of the gifts which can give the enemy grounds for attack, something to seriously consider. I say this because, in retrospect, I don't think that God told me to curse that plumbing, nor do I believe that the end result came out of God's will. That curse came out of a heart of judgment, not from the heart of God.

A prominent church leader north of where I live related a story of a prophet that spoke at a conference he was attending. He said that the prophet made a prophetic declaration regarding a specific disaster that would occur. Virtually the next day this disaster came to pass exactly as he said it would. A number of people died as a result. The following day the tragedy was reported in the paper, and it was announced at the same conference where it had been proclaimed. People rejoiced at God's judgment.

The leader (north of where I live) attending the conference was understandably angry. He later explained that he felt God had been misrepresented because people presume that because a person declares something, and it comes to pass, that somehow God willed it to happen or that the declaration itself is somehow divinely inspired. This leader went on to explain that this simply is not the case, and that *God's gifts and call are irrevocable.* He went on to say that people who are given a lot of spiritual authority can carry a lot of power in the spirit realm. This leader reasoned that the greater level of authority that a person carries in Christ, the more impact their words will have. The idea was that this spiritual authority is something every believer possesses in one degree or another, and that this spiritual truth can become very damaging if not understood and realized.

If what he is saying is true, then it stands to reason that spiritual authority can also serve to have a much greater positive impact if understood and actualized in the life of a believer. I would agree wholeheartedly with this respected leader. God has not called us to prophesy judgment but to proclaim His mercy and grace through Jesus Christ. Jesus didn't come to destroy men's lives but to save them (Luke 9:56). Our mission as Christians is always to be redemptive. Remember, our battle is not against flesh and blood, but spiritual forces of wickedness (Ephesians 6:12).

It is for this reason that every believer must **realize** their positional authority and the power that we possess in Christ.

Just as the believer's authority unrealized can be destructive, the believer's authority realized can be an unstoppable force for good and a powerful agent for healing and change. It is imperative that every believer recognize that God has given to each of us the authority to take back the earth and to bring it under kingdom rule. *".... to fill the earth and subdue it and rule over the creation"* (Genesis 1:28). Though Adam lost dominion over the earth momentarily to Satan, that dominion has since been restored through Jesus Christ. The issue with many Christians today is that they still believe they are powerless. Like many of the former slaves right after they were set free after the abolition of slavery, many still hold a slave mentality. Many freed slaves still felt powerless. Some even believed they were still slaves. It took quite some time before the mindset of the African American was able to catch up to their current reality. I think this mirrors the church in some ways. Jesus Christ's death, burial, and resurrection set us free from sin, gave us eternal life, and reinstated our dominion over the earth and the devil. Many Christians, however, still live in bondage to fear, playing it safe. Many fear taking risks, reluctant to stretch the boundaries of their faith, clinging to what is, for the most part, a purely historical, rational, and predictable Christianity.

God has called his church to take dominion of the earth by exercising authority over the devil, destroying fortresses, and demolishing strongholds of darkness. We've been called to suppress demonic influence by exercising our God-given kingdom authority over it. This kingdom authority is exercised through our spoken words. *"Death and life are in the power of the tongue; and they that love it shall eat of its fruit"* (Proverbs 18:21). Every believer has been given the authority and power to shape their future and destiny (James 3:2-4), alter their circumstances, and even change the physical reality. Now, some of you are reading this and thinking, "Is he serious?" Here is why I'm saying this. Consider that God created the heavens and the earth through His spoken word. God literally spoke the universe into existence. Then He created mankind in His image and gave them dominion over the earth. It's been mankind's commission from the beginning to subdue the earth. We do that *now* by bringing the rule and reign of Christ wherever we go, and by establishing the kingdom of God and His glory in places previously occupied by darkness. Mankind lost dominion because of words spoken (by the serpent's lies and man's belief in them). Conversely, Man also regains dominion over the earth through words spoken. Jesus said, *"Go into all the world and **preach the gospel** to all creation... "* (Mark 16:15-18). It is in the practice of speaking forth His word that we exercise our spiritual authority and take back what was lost by Adam.

DECLARATION AND DECREE

Noun
Declaration: The act of declaring: making a legal announcement.
Decree: An order usually having the force of law.

Another great weapon in our spiritual arsenal is declaration or decree. The practical way in which we take dominion over enemy influence and encampments is through declaration or decree. I will be using these words interchangeably throughout this chapter. Declarations or decrees made by a believer are audible words that have power on them. Your words carry power by virtue of your position in Christ alone. Kings make decrees because they are royalty, and those who are royalty rule. Because they rule, when they decree an edict or something else, it stands and is unchangeable. We as children of the King are part of a royal priesthood, a holy nation, a people that belong to God (1 Peter 2:9). We are sons and daughters of God. We are co-heirs with Christ (Romans 8:15-16). We rule and reign and are seated with Christ in heavenly realms (Romans 5:17, Ephesians 2:6). In other words, you have a special relationship with the King and that gives you a lot of clout in spirit realms. Moreover, your words not only carry a lot of weight initially, but the power of your words increases with the level of anointing that you are operating in at any given moment. Even if you feel no anointing at all, your words still have power and effect. Believe it!

One example of this spiritual power released through words took place some years ago, a few years after Lori and I were married. Now, I have a great marriage, and I think my wife and I are as well matched as any couple I have ever known. However, there was a season when our marriage came under severe attack. The kids were younger, and there seemed to be a growing animosity between Lori and me. This would manifest itself in arguments, long periods of silence, and an increasing feeling of distance in our relationship. The strange thing was the more that I tried to analyze and fix it, the worse it got. That was when it dawned on me that there was something spiritual going on, something I could not control or fix in the natural. I realized that my marriage was under spiritual attack.

One day I went to the Lord in prayer. As I prayed, the Lord brought to my attention that I had not been covering my marriage or my family in prayer. About this time, a friend had given me a book of declaration prayers called *"Praying with Fire"* by Barbara Billet. In it I found a number of Biblical declarations that one could make over the various areas of life. So I drove out to a place that I like to go to when I want to be alone. I turned to the marriage declaration and began to speak out loud. I began to decree God's word and His promises over my marriage and my family.

I began starting each morning with a declaration over my wife and kids. The changes I began to notice in our marriage were almost immediate. It confirmed to me that the enemy had in fact been targeting my marriage which gave me a resolve to be diligent in covering it. I began to also realize that the demonic was targeting every Christian marriage, and that one of Satan's high priorities is to destroy every marriage and family. Why? Because marriage and families are the backbone of any societal community. That may seem like a no-brainer to some of you, but for me the epiphany was that my words, spoken out loud in secret, could have an immediate impact on my circumstances, in this case my marriage. The changes that my declarations brought to my marriage were very obvious to me. For example, I noticed right away that communication between Lori and me was easier. The interference that previously seemed to be there was gone. That feeling of increasing distance was gone, and the warmth between us soon returned. Making decrees over my family brought such dramatic results that it opened my eyes to just how practical and useful spiritual warfare could be in our everyday lives. I noticed others struggling in their marriages and began sharing some of these principles with them. I soon began to witness other marriages being restored in the same way.

I also began to see changes in my kids. As I mentioned earlier in chapter 7, the kids argued in a different spirit. For a period of time, they were arguing constantly; moreover, the intensity of their hostility and their exchanges were mean-spirited and very angry. Hostility would build and crescendo into insults and hurt feelings. I was sensing an increasing divide between us as a family. Now, some might think that this hostility is normal for adolescents, and I might have been inclined to agree except for the fact that when I started making these decrees over my kids, I saw them change. When I started making the decrees over my family, I began to observe a number of changes almost immediately. The first thing I noticed was that communication was restored. As I stated before, the change wasn't that they didn't argue any more, they still did. However, now the meanness was gone. Relationship and a spirit of cooperation returned. I was now convinced that my time spent in the mornings declaring God's word over my family was not merely time well spent, but an imperative.

As I have been saying, our words have the power to change things. I am convinced that our words have the power to profoundly impact our physical reality and our future. I believe that the repetition of our spoken words has a direct and cumulative effect on our future experience and on our very lives as well. I'm not the only one saying this. Professors from Rutgers University and Yale reviewed a number of studies involving as many as 23,000 people and came to the conclusion that how people perceive themselves and how they speak and talk about their health will have a direct impact not just on their quality of health, but also on their longevity of life. The scriptures certainly support this truth when we read that *life and death are in the power of the tongue* (Proverbs 18:21).

I'm convinced that believers have the positional authority and the spiritual power to effect change not just in their own health, but also on physical reality by the use of their words. Dr. Masaru Emoto, a Japanese scientist, looked at how water crystals form as they begin to freeze, and the effect of the spoken word next to the water sample. As the water samples were frozen, those water samples that were spoken over with positive and kind words formed ice crystals with beautiful design and symmetry. Those water samples that had negative words or nothing spoken over them froze into ice that lacked symmetry or any kind of formation at all. This proved a consistent pattern throughout his experimentation.

I believe these findings support the principles outlined in this chapter. God has given to us as believers the power to impact, shape and even change our physical reality by declaring and decreeing His will and His word over a situation or circumstance. I remember one time that my elbow was experiencing severe tendonitis. I use my arm every day to check people for weapons who come through my gate at work. There was pain when I would bend it, but I knew the power of God's spoken word. So I began speaking over my health, over my body, and more specifically, my elbow. It didn't happen immediately, but it did happen- I was healed!

Because believers have authority and power as representatives of the King of all kings, Jesus Christ, their words also have the authority and power to effect changes on creation. This is because God gave man authority over the creation, and Jesus reversed the curse of Adam, restoring that authority back to mankind. The authority of the believer and the power of our words in the form of prophetic declaration and decree have limitless possibilities when you consider that God has called us to use our words to redeem the world!

Back in my college days I knew next to nothing about prophetic declaration, but I had a lot of faith for things. One time my friend Michael and I decided to go across the street to a neighboring college to witness to some of the students. When we got there, we noticed a very loud punk band had set up and was in concert in the middle of the campus. As the concert went on, we began to discern a darkness around the campus. For one thing, the music was dark and loud, and the lyrics were filled with obscenities. My friend discerned that the music was releasing demonic power into the atmosphere, thus hindering our efforts to reach people. Since it was an outdoor concert, my friend said, "Why don't we call down rain to stop this concert? Then we can witness to people". It was overcast, so we actually believed there was a chance God might do this. So, we began calling down the rain. After calling down rain for five minutes (five minutes is a long time) we both felt a sprinkle. We went ballistic! Our faith shot way up, and we got louder and started to shout the rain down! Then the rain started in steady. We were beside ourselves! We started to shout! More Lord! More Lord! As we shouted, the rain began to come in heavy. The more we asked, the heavier the rain came. To our amazement the band continued to play. They seemed unconcerned about their electrical equipment. The battle was on! We asked God for more, and the rain got heavier. The rain continued to pummel the band. Eventually, they just had to stop. The rain was just too heavy as the full-blown downpour continued. When the band finally stopped, Michael and I continued to walk the hallways of the campus meeting students and talking to them about Jesus.

The reason I share that story is to encourage believers to take bold and bodacious risks with their faith. You have nothing to lose. Step out and try things. You have an extravagant Father who is nuts about you! God has given us the ability and the power to shut down the enemy's influence in our world and in our individual spheres of influence. This authority is exercised through our words in declarations. The practice of making declarations has had an impact on my marriage, my family, my health, my church, ministry, as well as, finances. I am not more special than any other Christian. God is no respecter of persons. What God does for me he will do for any other Christian who believes in His word and His promises.

If every believer would take hold of what they have actually been given, we could change the world! That is not just a grandiose idea! I say that because it's true! Think about what would happen if every believer began to understand their identity in Christ and step into the authority that's been given to them. Imagine each believer taking authority over the enemy by taking away his right to act! Imagine each believer literally shutting down all demonic influence in their individual spheres of life, at work, in their schools, in their homes and in their families. Imagine the church coming together to take authority over the demonic activity that currently has influence over governments, cities, countries and the world! Imagine how the world would radically change if the demonic were not allowed to exercise influence. This is no pipe-dream. As sure as I have ever been about anything, I know this is possible! But it first must start in the church. Christians must overcome their fear and be willing to enter into battle and engage our enemy. Many believers still live in fear of spiritual power, spiritual gifts, spiritual warfare and the demonic. This is why it is important that every believer know that we do not battle alone, and neither are we alone in the world.

*I have included in the following pages of this chapter some sample declaration prayers that may be used in the various circumstances that people struggle with.

I encourage you to speak these out loud in faith. By virtue of God's faithfulness and promises, He will be true to His word. As you speak these out in authority, persevering in faith, you will find that your circumstances will begin to change.

MODEL DECLARATION
FOR THE BLOOD OF JESUS
(For cleansing or to deny the enemy rights or access)

*Today, I declare and decree that the Blood of Jesus
washes me from every sin and stain. Every fault, flaw,
weakness and sin has been erased and blotted out.*

*I declare that the Blood of Jesus justifies and makes
me righteous. Every sin and transgression is paid
for and rendered null and void in Jesus' name.*

*Today, the Blood of Jesus enables me to stand righteous
and justified before God. My whole body, soul, and spirit is
cleansed, washed and purged from all unrighteousness.*

*I am redeemed, sanctified, and purified from all defilement
by the precious Blood of Jesus. The Blood of Jesus delivers
me from all rights, grounds and dominion of darkness.*

*Today I plead the Blood of Jesus over my mind and
thought processes, over my memories and imagination.
My mind and thoughts are protected and sealed.*

*I plead the Blood of Jesus over my body. My
health and strength are restored.*

*Today I plead the Blood of Jesus over myself, my
family, and my property. Protect and cover all
that is mine by Your Blood, Lord Jesus.*

Thank You for the power of your Blood that allows me to come boldly before Your throne to find grace for help. Your Blood has given me access to Your presence and victory for life.

Thank you Lord for working all things together for good in my life because I am called according to Your good purpose and covered, sealed and preserved by Your Blood.

Praise You Lord! You are worthy to receive all glory honor and blessing, forever and forever—Amen!

MODEL DECLARATION
FOR COVERING YOUR MARRIAGE

Today, I bring my marriage before You Father, and I declare Your grace and blessing over my marriage. I thank you Father that the blood of Jesus cleanses us from all sin and stain. Thank you for forgiving us by your grace and mercy, as we also are forgiving one another in Jesus' name.

As You created the heavens and the earth and spoke it into existence, I know that you, Lord, are speaking into our marriage, renewing our marriage by the word of your power. As You speak Father, none of Your words will return void, and every word will accomplish that which you have purposed. Release Your Holy Spirit over our marriage this day in Jesus' name.

As we have entered into covenant with you and each other, I thank you, Lord, that we are kind and patient with each other, and that we defer to one another, that we are generous and self-sacrificing to each other. I thank You, Lord, that we walk as one and that You, Lord, are exerting Your Divine power and influence over our marriage in Jesus' name

In the mighty name of Jesus I come against the spirit of darkness, deception, dissension, factions and strife, gossip, slander, the religious spirit, the spirit of hypocrisy, rebellion and witchcraft, seduction, pornography, adultery and idolatry, and I decree that your power and influence over our marriage is broken, shattered and destroyed this day. I decree that any and all dark powers of influence against our marriage are cut off and dissolved. I break your power and render your assignment null and void in Jesus' name.

I decree that love, joy and peace shall rule over our marriage this day. I thank you, Lord, that we still love each other and that we are both kind, thoughtful, and considerate of one another.

Today I decree that all the weapons of hell, death and destruction shall not succeed against my marriage. No device, conspiracy, lie, tragedy, separation, disease or discord or divorce will prevail against us.

Thank You, Lord, for protecting and brooding over our marriage today. You are working, shaping, and molding us into perfect unity and understanding. Thank You, Father, for waging war on our behalf. You are bringing about strength and unity, love, peace, joy and respect again in our marriage. You are a great God, and I love you in Jesus' name.

MODEL DECLARATION
FOR FINANCES

Today I thank You, Father, for your love, grace and mercy. Thank You for being Jehovah Jireh my provider and for generously supplying me with every spiritual blessing in the heavenly realms. Today, I declare and decree that I am under the blessing of Abraham, and that my whole body, soul and spirit prospers in Jesus name.

I believe that God is able to do exceedingly above and beyond all that I could ask, think, or imagine in the name of Jesus. I am under God's blessing and favor. God is blessing everything I put my hands to. I am blessed in my coming in and my going out. I am blessed when I lie down and when I rise up.

I thank You, Lord, that as I have given, it will be given to me. Pressed down, shaken together and running over, it will be poured into my lap. Because I have been generous, people will go out of their way to be generous to me.

I come against the spirit of poverty and debt, and I break the power of your assignment over my life. I speak against the curse of poverty and debt, and I break, shatter and destroy the curse of poverty in Jesus' name.

Father, I rebuke the devourer, and I break the cycle of debt and neediness in Jesus name. I loose all burdens of poverty, debt and oppression and I command you to let go of my finances now in Jesus' name.

Today, I confess that I am debt-free and that I have no lack. The Lord is my shepherd, and I shall not want for anything.

I confess that God is overflowing my storehouses. He is overwhelming me with His blessings and His favor. He is making me a blessing that I might be a blessing to others. The Lord is rejoicing as He is pouring out His abundant supply on my life.

The Lord is giving me abundant favor, blessing, increase and wisdom over my finances. Thank You, Lord, for Your Divine counsel and wisdom and victory over my finances in Jesus' Name. Amen!

MODEL DECLARATION
FOR A REBELLIOUS CHILD

Father, I thank you that ____ is a blessing and a gift. I thank
You that ____is blessed coming in and blessed going out. I
thank You, Lord, that Your hand is on ____ 's life, and that
you are leading and guiding him/her, even bringing about
your discipline when necessary. You, Lord, are working,
exercising divine energy and influence on his/her behalf.
You, God, are molding and shaping ____, accomplishing
your intention and purpose in the name of Jesus.

I thank You Father that in the areas where I have failed as
a parent, You by Your grace, are making up the difference.
You are fathering and mothering them where needed. You
are bringing about your perfect plan on their behalf.

Father, since You have given me power over all the power of
the enemy, I take authority over the enemy on behalf of my
child____. In the name of Jesus, I bind every unclean spirit of
addiction, lust, seduction, pornography, idolatry, dissension,
factions and strife, gossip, rebellion, witchcraft, the religious
spirit, the spirit of hypocrisy, the fear of man, the fear of rejection,
lies, every prince or power of the air, I bind you and render you
powerless and ineffective against my child in Jesus' name!

Thank You, Father, for keeping ____safe from every device, trap,
conspiracy, lie and assignment of the enemy. Thank you for
keeping them away from every corrupting man, woman or spirit.

Lord, you said that no one can snatch your sheep out of your
hand. You are going before____ to wage war against the enemy

on his/her behalf. I ask that you give him/her divine wisdom, discernment and discretion. Fill him/her Lord with Your grace and understanding. I thank you that you are going forth to set him/her free. Thank you for saving, healing and delivering _____. I believe and confess that _____ is set free this day. Amen!

MODEL DECLARATION FOR DIVINE HEALTH AND HEALING OF THE BODY

Today, I bless my body from head to toe. In the name of Jesus, I renounce the curse of Adam. The Blood of Jesus cleanses me from all sin and defilement. The enemy has no more access or rights to my body. I am set free from the law of sin and death.

I declare and decree that I have divine health. My whole body, soul and spirit are consecrated and set apart for God's will and purposes. I am no longer under the bondage of sin and slavery. I am set free in mind and body. I decree that my whole body, soul and spirit are blessed with health and strength. My health is blessed even as my soul is blessed in the name of Jesus. In Jesus' name, my brain and nervous system fire and function according to God's purpose and design. There will be no swelling in the nerves, and no misfiring of signals in my nervous system. All pain will go in Jesus' name.

In the name of Jesus, my heart and circulatory system will function and operate according to God's purpose and design. My heart will pump blood effectively bringing oxygen and healing to my body. There will be no blocks or clogging in my arteries or veins. Everything will stretch and function as God intended it to function. There will be no dysfunction in my body in Jesus' name.

In Jesus' name every organ in my body will function according to God's purpose and intention. All my organs will be blessed with perfect operation. Every tumor and growth will break up, dissolve and pass through my body in Jesus' name.

Every bone and joint, tendon and ligament, every piece of cartilage and muscle tissue will function, move, and operate according to God's purpose and design. My bones, joints, and body are blessed with perfect health and strength.

In Jesus' name, my blood will attack, cleanse and purge my body of every virus, disease and germ. There will be no malfunction in my immune and limbic system. Everything in my immune system will function and operate according to God's perfect design. Thank You for blessing me with health and strength, Lord Jesus.

MODEL PRAYER
FOR A SPIRIT OF MIGHT

Pray this prayer for an increase in strength

Father, today I decree that I will be strong and courageous.
I will not be afraid, nor will I be dismayed.

Oh Lord my God, today I confess and decree by faith that I have
on the full armor of God. I am armed with Your Spirit of strength
and Your mighty power. I am empowered with might by my
union with You, O Lord. I am strengthened with might by Your
Spirit in the inner man today in the mighty Name of Jesus.

I decree that the Lord is my lamp. He illumines my
darkness. In God's strength I can crush an army. With God,
I can scale any wall. The Lord is a shield about me. He is
the strength of my life and the strength of my heart. The
Lord is my strong tower, my refuge, and my fortress.

I declare and decree that the Lord is my solid rock. My God arms
me with strength, and He makes my way perfect. He makes my
feet likes hind's feet, so that I can scale the mountain heights.
He trains my hands for war and my fingers for battle so that
my arms can bend a bow of bronze in the name of Jesus

Lord, you have given me your shield of victory, and Your right
hand supports me. Your help and gentleness make me great. You
have made a wide path for my feet to keep them from slipping.

I can defeat all spiritual forces of the evil one, for God is with
me. I will chase my enemies away. I will not stop till they are

conquered. I will destroy the works of the devil. I will strike them so they cannot get up. My foot will be upon the neck of my enemies, for you, O Lord, have girded me with strength for battle; You have subdued all my enemies in Jesus' Name.

I decree that the God has given me victory today. Therefore, I will live in peace on every side.

Thank you Lord for Your strength, Your power, and protection this day in Jesus' Name! Hallelujah!

CHAPTER 9

DEPLOYING ANGELS

"Then Elisha prayed and said, 'O Lord I pray, open his
eyes that he may see'. And the Lord opened the servant's
eyes and he saw; and behold, the mountain was full
of horses and chariots of fire all around Elisha."
2 Kings 6:17 NASB

Some time ago my family and I decided to go on a short term
mission trip to Haiti. We decided it would be a great experience
to serve together at some of the orphanages. That decision has
since led to a number of other trips over there. The first couple
of trips over were eye-opening. My wife and I volunteered to
help lead the teams that our church was sending. She would
handle the administration, and I would facilitate the evening
study and devotions for the group. We had learned from the
briefing on the first trip and our research that voodoo was
a big part of the culture as well as one of the major religious
practices. Now I am somewhat spiritually sensitive, so I was
curious as to what we would encounter on these trips.

As I said, the first couple of trips were full of surprises and
very eye opening. For instance, we travel in a group, and we
all wear the same T-shirt, so it's obvious we're a mission team.
The purpose of identical shirts was to help us all stay together
throughout the trip, but part of me felt that we all had targets

painted on our backs. At one of the airports where we had a stopover, one of our team members was all of a sudden overcome with weakness. She began to tremble and cry, sliding against the wall down to the floor. She said that she felt nauseous. As she crouched on the floor, it appeared that she was going to wretch. I considered where we were going and what we were intending to do and discerned that this was a spiritual attack. I asked a couple of the team members to pray with me for her. After praying the blood of Jesus over her and rebuking any spiritual attack, she recovered almost immediately and suffered no repercussions afterward. A few minutes later we were on the plane to Haiti, with our team-member feeling fine.

The mission in Haiti was also quite an experience. On our first two mission trips one of the resident missionaries (not one of our team members) was shot by bandits. She came to the orphanage where we were staying for medical treatment and to have the bullet extracted. On another occasion, a dog ran out in front of us and was struck and killed by our truck. This greatly upset the local Haitians. A group of them started calling out to us. We thought that they might get violent, but one of the local missionaries was able to settle the matter. On still another occasion, after our team left the site, a number of men armed with guns jumped the fence of the compound and held the missionaries at gunpoint in an execution style position on their knees while they went through the site stealing all their computers and other electronic equipment. They also managed to seize the orphanage's cash reserve of money. Travel was also problematic. When our team arrived at the airport to return home, the airport attendants wanted to split up our team which would have required half the team to spend another night in town. We immediately began to pray that God would intervene, and no sooner did we pray then the problem resolved itself, and we were able to all fly back together.

It was these kinds of challenges that got me to consider terraforming our third mission's trip and especially our team members. Terraforming also involves the practice of calling on God for angelic assistance. I figured that if Jesus could appeal to Father for twelve legions of angels (Matthew 26:53), then I could appeal for a few as well. After all, where does it say that you can't? Now, I know from my studies that in the first century, one legion equaled 6000 soldiers. So, I knew twelve legions would be a lot of angelic might. I also considered that Haiti was a place where we would need to far outnumber our spiritual adversaries. No need to worry about exhausting heaven of all its angelic hosts. The scriptures say that the angels of God are tens of thousands of thousands of thousands (Psalm 68:17). Plenty of angels in heaven!

So, before our next trip I began to appeal to God for several legions of angels to escort us to and from Haiti. Consequently, this trip went much smoother with no adverse incidents as before. Travel even went off without a hitch. I'm convinced that our angelic escorts were not only present, but were also very attentive to any needs that arose on our trip. We left and returned without incident and have had no incidents since then.

For most of my Christian life angels were somewhat of a fairy tale, certainly nothing I gave any thought to. Oh, I believed in them, but they didn't seem to have any relevance to my life personally. I thought it was nice if they were around but never really understood the role that they potentially played in my life and in my walk with God. One of the greatest discoveries I've made in my personal walk with God is the deploying of angels. In the past I never considered this, but over the last few years I have found that I can call on Father to send angels for very specific tasks.

This next weapon of spiritual warfare is nothing short of awesome and is rarely if ever used by Christians. This is the deployment of angels for protection and assistance in spiritual warfare. The scriptures indicate that as believers, we will one day judge angels (1Corinthians 6:3). The scriptures even tell us that the specific purpose of angels is to minister and render service to those who are Christians (Hebrews 1:14). Nonetheless, angels are to be respected and revered. I would never consider it appropriate to bark out orders or command angels to do anything. They are far more powerful than we are. Remember that it only took one angel to wipe out 185,000 Assyrian soldiers (2 Kings 19:35). Having said that, I do believe we have the ability and the access to appeal to our Father for angels. This is nothing new. Others have been doing this for quite some time, but for some reason I always thought they had a special gift or something I didn't have. What I came to realize is that any believer has access to these angelic majesties through our Father.

The first time I began using angelic assistance was at the end of a deliverance ministry session to help a person get free from demonic bondage and strongholds. Our bodies are considered to be temples of God, and often I would call to God to dispatch warring angels to rout the enemy and sweep His temple clean. Angels can be helpful in deliverance because they will expose any demonic remnant missed or overlooked. Another application of this is in the workplace. In one of the previous chapters on Terraforming, I focused on taking away the rights of the demonic. When demonic powers no longer have the grounds to act, then I will call in the angels to sweep out any and all demonic strongholds, stumbling blocks and pockets of resistance in my workplace. This has proven to be extremely effective because once the enemy loses grounds to carry out their agenda; angels are empowered to remove any interference made by the enemy. This applies regardless of location. As I have mentioned earlier in this book, I have experienced dramatic changes in my work environment when I have Terraformed my workplace and called in angels. Deploying angels is the final blow to dark powers in any context of spiritual warfare, but especially in Terraforming.

I have called in angels when we were experiencing turbulent times as a family relationally and emotionally. This always made a profound difference in the restoration of peace to our home during those seasons.

Another application for the deployment of angels is for the protection of property. In Psalm 127:1 we read, *"Unless the Lord guards the city, the watchman keeps awake in vain."* Remember when Jesus said that the thief (devil) comes to steal, kill, and destroy (John 10:10). Stealing and destroying are a big part of our enemy's agenda, often manifesting as vandalism, theft, and the destruction of property. Deploying of angels can prevent this. My wife and I often organize and lead activities for our church. We often plan group hikes. One time we had planned a hike for our group. On this occasion we had decided to hike at a place that had very limited parking at the trailhead. This particular site had a notorious reputation for car break-ins and vandalism. To make matters worse, when we got there we noticed broken pieces of windshield glass all over the ground. This didn't make everybody real keen on the hike. So, we joined hands to pray before we decided to step out on the trail, something we do routinely, asking for safety. This time, though, I asked God to station warring angels around the cars and to protect our property. We were gone all day, and later when we got back our cars remained untouched and undisturbed. Moreover, numerous times we have hiked in such places and to date we have never had a single break-in to any car.

It is my conviction that most theft and vandalism is demonically instigated and can be prevented by taking the time to pray and request Father for angels to stand watch. If the enemy comes to steal, then the demonic is about stealing. Angels can scare away and deflect any kind of demonic ploy to rip you off! This totally makes sense to me, and my faith in God has grown in this area. I believe that my property is safer with my Father's angelic guardians then with all the locks in Fort Knox. We need to always remind ourselves, *"Unless the Lord guards the city, the watchman keeps awake in vain."* Now I am not saying that you should stop locking your house or your car or valuables. God naturally expects us to use wisdom and common sense, but asking God for angels can only help.

Another subject that needs even more serious consideration regarding the deployment of angels is the protection of life. I absolutely believe that all the mass shootings that we hear about in the news are demonic in their impetus. By that I mean that these acts are inspired and driven by demons. Few if any believers would argue with that. These acts are inhuman. It's my conviction that demons gain access to a human host through some doorway that the host was involved in previously. This gives the demon control or at least strong influence over the person. It's the demon that uses the host to carry out its blood lust. That doesn't mean that the person isn't responsible or that they shouldn't be made accountable for their actions, but we need to remember that our battle is not against flesh and blood. The enemy's agenda is not only to steal but to kill as well. If this is true, then it makes sense that a number of angelic guards could detour or prevent these things from happening.

If this is the case, then it also stands to reason that the shooting rampages like the one at the movie theater in Aurora, or the shooting in Columbine High School in Colorado, and others shootings theoretically could have been prevented by mindful believers praying in angelic protection. But the church must first take on a warfare mentality, realizing that we are in a war, and that our enemies are dark spirits.

Now some might ask, "Aren't there angels around anyway? Couldn't God have intervened if He wanted to? Wouldn't angels act on their own if they wanted to?" These are valid questions. My answer to these questions is that for some reason that I may never understand, God has chosen to use His church to intercede on behalf of the world. It is our prayers, petitions and declarations that move the hand of God to make a difference in the world around us. It's my own prayers and decrees that have proven this to be true, which is why I am writing this book. I'm writing to help other believers to realize the potential difference they can make as they learn to successfully operate in spiritual warfare, exercising their spiritual authority. Angels are just one of many resources the believer has at their disposal.

Many think of angels as they are often depicted in the old Rembrandt paintings, where they are seen as children with short little wings. The reality however, is that angels can be terrifying and awesome to behold (Matthew 28:3-4). This means that if they are deployed at the request of one of Christ's servants, it can potentially mean the difference between life and death in some cases. However, preventive warfare means never having to find out. We may never know what the preventive actions of deploying angels in our workplace or our children's schools may have stopped or prevented if we are diligent in covering such places in our prayers. I do know, however, that I have personally witnessed significant changes in my workplace when I have been intentional about deploying angels to protect my co-workers and stand guard over the entrance to our facility. The success of deploying angels for protection is predicated on first removing the enemy's rights to act or to operate in the particular place being prayed over. The removal of the demonic's grounds to operate in any location is done through Terraforming. Then angels can be very effective. If demons have the rights to operate in any social or public setting, then angels will not be nearly as effective. Any social or public setting must first be cleansed with the blood of Jesus and the sins of the people remitted before angels are deployed. Then the angelic is empowered to carry out the request of the believer's appeal to God.

Calling down angelic assistance and protection is another best-kept secret in Christendom. There is a true story that perfectly illustrates this reality. It took place in the 1950's during the Korean War. The account was written in a letter by a young Marine to his mother. US Navy Chaplain Father Walter Muldy talked to the Marine and his mother to get a first-hand account of the incident. He also interviewed the young Marine's commander to confirm the story's credibility.

The Chaplin later read this Marine's original letter to a gathering of 500 at a Navy Base in San Diego, California, to help the listeners better relate to the incident from this Marine's perspective. The letter reads as follows:

Dear Mom,

I am writing to you from a hospital. Don't worry mom, I'm ok. I was wounded, but the doctor says that I will be up in no time.

But this isn't why I'm writing. Something happened to me that I wouldn't dare tell anyone but you, because no one would believe it. In fact, you may even find it hard to believe, but I just have to tell you anyway.

Remember the prayer to St. Michael that you urged me to pray before I left to Korea, Michael of the morning? Well I prayed it...Every day.

Well, one day we were out on patrol looking for enemy soldiers. I had been patrolling for some time before I suddenly noticed that there was this huge Marine walking right next to me.

I started talking to him. I found it strange that I had never met him before when I knew everyone well in my unit.

I said, "I thought I knew everyone in my unit, but I never met you." In which he replied, "No, I've just joined. The name is Michael."

"Really? That's my name too!"

"I know," the big Marine said. "Michael, Michael of the morning." He knew the first line of my prayer Mom!

Well, it was very cold and it started to snow. I noticed that I could see my breath in the cold air, but I couldn't see any breath coming out of this stranger's mouth.

Suddenly, he said to me, "There's going to be trouble ahead." Then he said, "It's going to clear up soon."

All of a sudden, the snow cleared, and we were standing face to face with enemy soldiers.

I dove for cover and yelled at the stranger to get down, but the big Marine just stood there, still and unphased. Bullets were flying everywhere. There was no way those soldiers could have missed him at that distance.

Well, I jumped up to pull him down, and that's when I got hit. I could feel pain in my chest. My head swam, and I could feel strong arms around me laying me down gently in the snow.

Then the stranger stood back up. I was dazed, but I opened my eyes. Michael's countenance seemed to radiate like the sun, and there was a terrible splendor in his face. The splendor increased around him like the wings of an angel. As I began to slip from consciousness, I saw that Michael held a sword in his hand. The sword flashed with a blinding light.

Later, when I woke up, the sergeant and all the guys kept asking me, "How did you do it?"

I asked them where Michael was, but the sergeant seemed confused and asked, "Michael who?"

"Michael, the big Marine who was walking with me." Then the sergeant replied, "Son you're the only Michael in this unit. Besides there was no one walking with you. I saw you. You were walking a little too far from us so I was watching, but you were alone. Now tell me how you did it?"

There was that question again. Now I was bugged. "How did I do what?!"

"How did you kill all those soldiers strewn all around you? There wasn't a single shot fired from your rifle, and each man was killed by a sword stroke."

That's my story. I don't know how it happened Mom, but there is one thing I'm absolutely sure about. It happened.

This Marine was given angelic protection simply because he asked for it. Now I am not advocating that any one should pray to the saints or even to the angels. However, I would like to encourage any believer who has need to petition your heavenly Father for angelic assistance when subduing spiritual forces of darkness. Jesus said, *"You have not because you ask not"* (James 4:2). *"Ask and it shall be given, seek and you will find, knock and the door shall be opened"* (Matthew 7:7). Angelic assistance is a believer's benefit that is largely untapped by the church community. We are not required to do warfare alone. Divine assistance is always available for the asking, and it has proven to be very effective to me personally.

I want to end this chapter by challenging you to experiment with this. For example, you may happen to currently be in a hostile work environment. First, Terraform your workplace, and then start petitioning God to send in an appropriate number of angels to subdue the demonic and to stand watch over your workplace. Deploying angels is not only an effective weapon of spiritual warfare, but it will significantly alter the atmosphere. Here is a sample prayer showing how to do just that.

MODEL PRAYER FOR DEPLOYING ANGELS

Father, I thank you for your love, mercy, grace, and compassion on us. I ask you to forgive all our sins, and to cover us in the blood of Jesus.

I plead the blood of Jesus over each and every person in my workplace. I plead the blood of Jesus over every person, place, and thing in my workplace, and over the very land itself.

I ask You, Father, to cleanse wash and purge us from all unrighteousness and to wash away all defilement of evil. Bring your light into every person, place and thing, and dispel all darkness in Jesus name

I ask you, Lord, to fill my workplace with Your Presence, and to establish your kingdom, Your rule, and reign in our midst.

Father, I ask you to loose your heavenly hosts to wage war on behalf of my co-workers. I ask you, Lord, to bring (pray about how many) number of Your angels to shut down all of the enemy's activity and influence.

I ask you, Lord, to shut down all rumors and remove the spirit of gossip, slander, dissensions, factions, division, and strife. Remove the spirit of pride and arrogance, rebellion and witchcraft, lust and idolatry. Break the power of the political and religious spirit. Bind up every spirit that is contrary to you, Lord, and send them away in Jesus' name.

I ask that You station your warring angels within and around the property so that Your kingdom will be established in my workplace in the name of Jesus.

Thank You, Father, for answering my petition and I give you all the glory this day in Jesus' mighty name. Amen!

CHAPTER 10

FAITH – YOUR SHIELD & ARMOR

"...In addition to all, taking up the shield of
faith with which you will be able to extinguish
all the flaming arrows of the evil one."
Ephesians 6:15 NASB

One of the greatest and most prized spiritual weapons of warfare for the believer is our shield and our armor. In the natural, soldiers and marines use body armor to protect themselves from bullets, bayonets, bombs, and all kinds of flack, anything that might inflict a fatal wound. It is body armor that has proven to save many a man in combat. This is also true spiritually.

Let's return to my workplace. Working at the courthouse can be interesting. You see people in all different states of mind. Some come in happy. Some come in or leave sad, even to the point of tears. Some come in disturbed, confused, angry, bitter, and hostile. Some are stoic and serious, some are extremely fearful, some are hurt. Some people are very arrogant and feel very superior. Some are humble and yet very classy. Some are very professional, and some are homeless. The point is that there is this diverse spectrum of humanity in the courthouse every day and few of them are having a great day. Consequently, some people can be quite reactionary to the circumstances in which they find themselves. This attitude is often manifest in their speech, which is often vented onto the resident guards working the gates. This is why, if you work the lobby as I do, you have to have a reasonably thick skin and not take things too personally.

The reality is that the human condition is such that the demonic can often access a person. Let's face it, most people are dealing with some kind of brokenness, and it's this brokenness that often gives access to the enemy. It's the demonic that uses their human host to shoot off these fiery darts in the form of harsh words spoken. These fiery darts come at us as harsh words spoken with energy on them (demonic power). These words can strike, penetrating us on a soulish level if we are not prepared. It is then that words can fester in our hearts and create all kinds of angst. This, in turn, can lead to bitterness. Bitterness, if left unchecked over a long period of time, can lead to all forms of physical maladies and conditions, including cancer. It is true that even as words can be used to bless, that they can also be used to curse, afflict and in extreme cases, even kill. So, the old adage, "sticks and stones may break my bones, but words can never hurt me," is simply not true. Most of us know at least one person who has grown up in a verbally abusive household and know of the profound impact harsh words made in that person's life, perhaps even yours.

It's for this very reason that God has given each member of His church body a shield and armor to protect and insulate our soul and spirit from demonic darts, arrows and missiles. These attacks often come in the form of words designed to bring down believers leaving us ineffective, if not wounded. I have divided these demonic weapons into three specific categories because this is what I do (ask my wife). So, I see three different levels of attack and have categorized them accordingly. Each level of attack becomes more personal and damaging. These categories are darts, arrows and missiles, each having differing degrees of power.

Darts – A demonic dart would be considered a relatively minor affliction and would involve unwarranted criticism, teasing, or joking at someone else's expense.

Arrows – Arrows are a little larger and more powerful than darts. These are more personal in nature and can involve labeling, name-calling or mocking.

Missiles - Missiles are extremely personal and are intended to destroy or cause damage, worry and fear. These involve vitriol, curses, threats, or bad reports.

These weapons of the enemy can prove formidable when we fail to properly clothe ourselves in the armor God has generously provided for us. Let's face it; some of us have more hurts, wounds, and brokenness than others. These past hurts, if not healed through ministry, can make us more vulnerable to attack, thinner- skinned, and much more sensitive to the words of others. But I have some great news! God has not left us without a way to defend ourselves.

Now most of us are familiar with Ephesians chapter 6 and putting on the armor of God. This passage of scripture is a fantastic gift to the believer for a number of reasons. First of all, it is a ready-made declaration which I have provided at the end of this chapter. But first let's look at these pieces of armor, starting with the helmet of salvation and working our way down.

Helmet of Salvation – In high school my football coach was teaching us how to block other players to protect our quarterback. I remember him once telling us to make sure that we control our opponent's head because where the head goes the body follows. That always stuck with me, because the same is true spiritually. Where our mind goes, the body soon follows. The enemy knows this, and that is why it is so important that we wear our helmet. The helmet of salvation denotes a mind that is fixed on the things of God. It is a mind fixed heavenward. It is focused on kingdom thinking and kingdom living. The scriptures encourage the believer to *"set your mind on the things that are above, not on earthly things"*(Colossians 3:2). Our helmet protects our thought life, and is applied by faith as we declare, "I put on the helmet of salvation." Believe me, those few words spoken audibly can make a big difference in how you think that day. The helmet of salvation is critical because it guards the mind from lies and false perceptions. The helmet is a mind with a view of God's kingdom and His purposes.

Breastplate of Righteousness – In the Marine Corps we were required to wear body armor in training or combat situations to protect us from the three Bs, bullets, bayonets, bombs and all kinds of flack. It's this body armor that protects your vital organs. Spiritually, it's the breastplate that protects your heart, the seat of your emotions. This is why God's word encourages us to *"guard our hearts with all diligence, for out of it flow the issues of life"* (Proverbs 4:23). It is the eyes of your heart that enable you to see in the spirit (Matthew 5:8) giving you prophetic vision and enabling you to hear God's voice. The breastplate of righteousness is important because it protects your dreams, your passion for the kingdom, and your vision given to you by God.

Shield of Faith – The Shield of Faith is our faith in the character of God. It's our faith in God's predisposition and His favor toward us. Job had a hedge of protection around him, and the enemy was unable to touch him. We as believers have that same hedge or shield of protection unless, of course, a person is giving the enemy grounds to attack. It's true that Job gave the enemy no grounds for the attack he experienced, but as I said earlier, Job was the exception to the rule, being an exceptional man by any standard. I would never assume that I would be worthy enough to undergo the kind of testing Job had to endure. The point is we have a shield, and this shield is the favor of God on your life. The shield is acquired by our faith in God's faithfulness, love, and favor upon us. It is this favor of God that extinguishes and vanquishes all the fiery darts, arrows, and missiles of the demonic.

Sword of the Spirit – The Sword of the Spirit is the believer's primary offensive weapon against the devil. This is the word of God. It is the audible word of God coming from your lips and is never to be used to attack people. We must always keep in mind that our battle is spiritual. The sword of the Spirit is specifically the word of God's truth spoken into a situation to break, dismantle, and destroy demonic strongholds created by lies, thus setting the captives free from demonic bondage. Power is released when we declare and decree God's word, God's truth, and God's promises. Authority and power are released when the believer declares God's truth into the air in spite of the circumstances. Such a declaration of faith puts things into motion in the spirit realm which, in turn, impacts the physical reality. The decreeing of God's word dismantles demonic strongholds and fortresses like addictions, witchcraft, generational curses, and rebellion.

It's when we resist the demonic that it leaves (James 4:7). Much of this book is dedicated to equipping the believer with a working knowledge of how to use the sword of God's word, encouraging Christians to displace the demonic by speaking God's truth in ministry situations and even into their various circumstances and environments to change atmospheres.

Belt of Truth – The belt of truth ties everything together. It has to do with your integrity. Truth is about holiness and holy living. We want to remain unstained by sin. Keep short accounts with God. This helps you to keep the fullness of God's anointing longer, and integrity helps to prevent leaks or dissipation of God's presence in your life.

Each of these pieces of spiritual weaponry is critical to the battle we are in. If you work in any secular environment you will inevitably bump into people's "stuff," their woundedness, their hurts, their demons. Such issues will often manifest in the workplace as negative vibes, attitudes and words. If you happen to be working in an openly hostile environment it's likely that the demonic has free range to operate. It's in these settings that applying your spiritual armor becomes critical and imperative. The fact is Christians should be armed every day. It's just that it often takes a lot of adversity to get us to realize that we actually need the armor! However, many believers do not know how to use what God has provided for them. It is for this reason that many feel beat up spiritually and emotionally if not defeated altogether.

The great news is that the armor can be easily applied simply by declaring and decreeing Ephesians 6:10-17 over yourself daily. The difference this makes is significant. I have been working in a government facility, specifically a high traffic public area for eight years. I can tell you from experience that applying the armor has given me a noticeably thicker skin emotionally and relationally. Before I began applying the armor or knew anything about spiritual warfare, I was much more easily agitated. Things seemed to get under my skin much more easily. Words would seem to fester, and I had more difficulty letting go of offenses. Much of this was because of words spoken that I now understand were empowered by the enemy. These fiery arrows would fill me with angst, and I would take things home with me and dwell on them – even occasionally losing sleep because of words exchanged with a co-worker or a supervisor. Now I have a very strong work ethic, and I consider myself to be fairly easy going and easy to get along with, so this wasn't normal for me. Therefore, I immediately began seeking to understand the spiritual dynamics behind my relationships at work.

As I mentioned earlier, I learned to Terraform and deploy angels in my workplace and in my home as well. So I came to discover during this same season that I could apply the armor of God much the same way I was Terraforming, binding demons or deploying angels: through declaration and decree. By audibly declaring the full armor of God over myself daily, I began to experience a much greater resistance against negative words spoken. These demonic darts, arrows and missiles were no longer having their intended effect. Negative words, though never pleasant, seemed to bounce off me instead of penetrating and festering in my soul.

I arrived at still another epiphany: the armor of God described in Ephesians 6 is much more than a mere analogy or metaphor. I started to understand that this armor was illustrating a literal spiritual armor to be put on and worn, and that it had to be worn on a daily basis. Ok, some of you are saying to yourselves, *"Duh, David, I knew that!"* Maybe you did, but I always took it to mean something a little less concrete and literal. Also, how it was to be put on and worn seemed to somehow elude me in the past. I began to understand that it was like putting on my pants or my shirt in the morning before I go to work. I needed to also put on each piece of spiritual body armor by declaring and decreeing it over myself. When I did this audibly by faith, I experienced a much greater resistance and resilience to spiritual attack. This small step has proven to make all the difference in the world in terms of my vulnerability to the enemy's attack! This practice is absolutely necessary for every believer's weapons arsenal, so I have provided a sample declaration that you can use.

PUTTING ON THE ARMOR OF GOD

*Thank you, Father, that I am strong in the
Lord and in the power of Your might.*

*I put on the full armor of God. I am able to stand firm, resolute and
immovable in the full strength of Your might, Lord, and I render
null and void all schemes, devices and conspiracies of the evil one.*

*Today, I come against all principalities, rulers, powers, forces of
darkness and all spiritual forces of wickedness in the heavenly
places, and I bind you and take you captive in Jesus' Name. I render
all your activities, plans and purposes null and void in Jesus' name.*

*I gird my core with truth and strength. I put on the breastplate
of righteousness. I am the righteousness of God in Christ Jesus.*

*I shod my feet with the gospel of peace
that my steps will be made sure.*

*I take up my faith as a shield. I extinguish all fiery darts,
arrows and missiles of the evil one, and I command
them to fall to the ground powerless in Jesus' name.*

*I put on the helmet of salvation, and I take up the
sword of the Spirit, that I may declare and decree
God's word, in the mighty Name of Jesus.*

CHAPTER 11

HEALING PRAYER

"And as you go, preach, saying, 'the kingdom of heaven is at hand.' Heal the sick, raise the dead, cleanse the lepers, cast out demons. Freely you received, freely give."
Matthew 10:7-8 NASB

Sam (not his real name) was in his early 60s. He came to us to get ministry for his neck. I was part of a ministry team at this time. He explained that some time ago he had had an accident which seriously injured his neck. He had surgery and, at the time he came to us, had been living with multiple pins in his neck. As a result, he was experiencing extreme pain in his neck and had no mobility. For example, if he attempted to turn his head he would have to move his shoulders and torso to look right or left. When he sat down, I asked him what his pain threshold was on a scale of 1 to 10 to get some perspective on what God would be doing. (This is something we often practice when doing ministry for a physical healing). He told us that it was an 8, very painful. I then asked Sam to move his neck as much as he could without moving his shoulders. His movement was practically nil; he was unable to move.

As we began to pray for Sam, I prayed the blood of Jesus over his neck, and I asked God to consecrate this part of his body. I then invited the Holy Spirit to begin to minister His healing touch. Then I spoke to the neck commanding it to be healed in Jesus' name. I said, *"I command the neck to be healed in Jesus' name. I command all the vertebrae to line up in Jesus' name, and I command the neck and vertebrae to be loosed in Jesus name! I command all parts in the neck to function as God created them to function, and I command all pain to leave now in Jesus name!"* Then we took a moment to see how Sam was doing. We asked him to try to turn his head. He attempted to turn his head and was able to move it ever so slightly and had about 20 percent of his mobility back. He also said that the pain was down to about a 6. Boy, were we excited! Our faith increased so much more in that moment! We continued to pray and bless what God was doing with Sam. After a short while, Sam was able to move his head side to side with 70 percent of his full range back. He told us that his pain was also down significantly. God was moving! We continued to pray, believing for Sam's complete healing and recovery. By the end of the session Sam had no pain and His full range of motion had increased to the point where he was able to turn his head at 90 degree angles both left and right. It was an amazing miracle of God, and we were thanking Jesus for His ministry and His healing touch!

It is an exciting moment when God begins to move in such a dramatic way. Healing is a way every believer can be used of God to dismantle the works of the enemy in a person's life. I want to address the subject of healing as a spiritual weapon at this time. For centuries the dark forces of this world have been afflicting mankind with sickness, disease and all various forms of infirmity. The devil comes to steal, kill and destroy, and he does this to a great extent by attacking a person's physical health. Jesus came to destroy the works of the devil. Jesus came to bring salvation and healing. Jesus came that we might have life and that more abundantly and fully. It has always been God's intention to save, heal, deliver, give life, restore and build up. These elements all together make up God's plan of redemption for mankind here on earth. And God has called His church to participate in His divine plan. Healing is one of the primary spiritual weapons given to the church. Healing was one of the primary ways that Jesus destroyed the devil's works. Healing is Christ's redemptive power made manifest in the physical realm. Jesus came to save the whole man. In other words, He came to redeem us body, soul and spirit.

One of the foremost ways the believer can undo the works of the devil is through the ministry of healing. Healing is a core component of Christ's ministry, and yet it is ignored by a significant portion of the church today. Healing prayer is one way we can participate in God's plan to reverse curses, release people from past pain, and heal their various afflictions and maladies. Many well-intentioned Christians are deceived into thinking that they are not called to heal the sick. Many feel unworthy to be used, or they think that healing is a special gift or calling for only a rare few. Still others don't believe that God would use us to heal at all, and that healing was something strictly for the first century church to get it established. Sadly, some embrace powerless theology, while propagating a powerless gospel, and in this the devil rejoices! He knows that a powerless church will never change the culture, shake the world or threaten Satan's kingdom.

This is why it is important to recognize what Jesus practiced throughout His life. As we look to the scriptures, we see that the earthly ministry of Jesus centered on three different activities: preaching the kingdom of God, healing the sick and casting out demons. Jesus, our ultimate example, modeled exactly the kind of ministry He intended to replicate in His disciples. They, in turn, were to teach others to do the "work of ministry."

Jesus said, *"As the Father sent me, I also send you"* (John 20:21). In other words, as Jesus operated and functioned in the world, so it was intended that His disciples were to likewise operate and function. Jesus said, *"All authority has been given to me in Heaven and on earth. Go, therefore, and make disciples of all nations teaching them to observe **all** that I have commanded you and lo, I am with you always...."* (Matthew28:18-20). Christ suffered, died, and was resurrected to redeem mankind and take back what had been lost through Adam. Then Christ recommissioned mankind through His church to once again subdue the earth. This simple truth establishes our spiritual authority to heal the sick and undo the works of the devil.

Not only that, but Jesus also gave us a model of discipleship to follow. Consequently, Jesus Christ is our blueprint for discipleship. He was the prototype, and as He functioned, so we are to function. We know this based on the commonsense principles of leadership training. For example, doctors have interns who learn to operate and function just as the doctors instruct and model them to do. Mechanics also have apprentices who learn to do things exactly as they are modeled and instructed to do. Jesus, being far wiser, certainly understood this basic principle of training others.

JESUS GIVES HIS MISSION STATEMENT

Jesus starts out by announcing His purpose and mission in the synagogue by reading out of Isaiah 61 in Luke 4:18-19. *"The Spirit of the Lord is upon Me, because He has anointed Me to preach the Gospel to the poor, He has sent Me to proclaim release* to the captives, and recovery of sight to the blind, to set free those who are downtrodden, to proclaim the favorable year of the Lord......" NASB Jesus stopped reading there, but the book of Isaiah goes on to say, *"And the day of vengeance of our God,* (God's vengeance is against the work of Satan by the hands of men and women. It is the church, commissioned by Christ that is undoing the works of the devil).

Isaiah continues: *"To comfort all who mourn....giving them a garland instead of ashes, the oil of gladness instead of mourning, The mantle of praise instead of a spirit of fainting, So they will be called oaks of righteousness, The planting of the Lord that He may be glorified. Then they will rebuild the ancient ruins. They will raise up former devastations and they will rebuild the ruined cities, the desolations of many generations...But you will be called the priests of the Lord, You will be spoken of as ministers of our God. You will eat the wealth of nations...Instead of shame you will have a double portion, and instead of humiliation they will shout for joy over their portion."* NASB

Everything in this passage has to do with healing, redemption, and restoration. We the church are to continue Christ's ministry by fulfilling His mission as it is declared in Isaiah. That is what Jesus did, and that is what He expects us to do as His disciples.

JESUS TRAINS AND EQUIPS OTHERS TO DO THE WORK OF MINISTRY

Jesus then does an interesting thing. He begins to multiply Himself by training and commissioning others. **First He commissions the twelve in Luke 9:1-2, 6.**

> *"And He called the twelve together, and gave them power and authority over all the demons and to heal diseases.*

> And He sent them out to proclaim the kingdom of God
> and to perform healing...And departing they began
> going about among the villages, preaching the gospel
> and healing everywhere." NASB

Later, Jesus commissions the seventy disciples in Luke 10: 1, 9, and 17

> "Now after this the Lord appointed seventy others, and
> sent them out two by two ahead of Him to every city and
> place He Himself was going to come. And He was saying
> to them...heal those who are sick and say to them, the
> kingdom of God has come near you...."

> "And the seventy returned with joy saying, Lord even
> the demons are subject to us in Your name. And He was
> saying to them, I was watching Satan fall like lightning.
> Behold I have given you authority to tread upon serpents
> and scorpions and over all the power of the enemy, and
> nothing shall injure you." NASB

**After His resurrection, Jesus commissions one hundred
and twenty disciples,** (Acts 1:15) empowering them by
sending the Holy Spirit on Pentecost Acts 2.

On the day of Pentecost God empowers His church and in
fulfilment of Joel 2:28 releases a prophetic movement like the
world has never seen (Acts 2:17-18). The church is released and
empowered to do the miraculous and to heal.

It's important that we understand that healing and
miracles were not just for the twelve as some may be inclined
to think. That is why, as followers of Christ, we need to know

who we are, as well as, whose we are. Our identity and the way we see ourselves has a direct impact on how we function in ministry and in the world.

UNDERSTANDING IDENTITY TRANSLATES INTO ROLE AND FUNCTION

If you see yourself as a Child of God then it becomes easy to trust and remain dependent on God. (Presuming that you had a healthy relationship with your parents and have a healthy understanding of what that relationship is like). Children are completely dependent on their parents. Children trust easily. The function of trust and dependence is directly related to the role of a child.

In the same manner, being a Son or Daughter of God gives you very special and intimate relationship with the Father (Romans 8:14-16). You begin to relate to God with the understanding that you have special favor and privilege because of that relationship. As Sons and Daughters of the King we are seated with Christ and ruling and reigning with Him (Ephesians 2:6). Identifying ourselves as Sons and Daughters of a reigning King makes us Princes and Princesses. As part of this royal line we can begin to exercise our rule and authority over spiritual darkness, sickness and disease, breaking the power of hell over the planet. We begin to step into our call to exercise our dominion over the demonic realm.

"But you are a chosen race, a royal priesthood, a holy nation, a people for God's own possession that you may proclaim the excellencies of Him who has called you out of darkness and into His marvelous light" 1Peter 2:9.

As royal priests we can understand that our role and function in the world is to act as mediators between God and an unbelieving world, snatching those out of the enemy's grasp as we limit demonic influence.

Jesus Christ came as Prophet, Priest and King. We as His representatives have been delegated to exercise and enforce His rule and reign, taking back what was lost. Your special relationship and position with God gives you that privilege, authority, favor and blessing. It is this reality that allows us to release God's divine healing to the hurting and the broken as we depend on the Holy Spirit.

JESUS MODELS DEPENDENCE ON THE HOLY SPIRIT

Jesus, our model for healing ministry, lived a life completely dependent on the Holy Spirit. He did this leaving us an example to follow. It's important to understand that Jesus, although He was fully and completely God incarnate, chose to limit Himself as a man. Consequently, Jesus never operated out of His divinity. Rather, He modeled (for us) a life completely dependent on the Holy Spirit to hear from the Father and to operate in all the spiritual gifts. We know this because Jesus, from time to time, expressed his limitations. In the gospel of Luke, chapter 8 we read about Jesus encountering a tormented and demonized man living among the tombs. Crying out with a loud voice, the demoniac spoke, *"What do I have to do with You Jesus, Son of the Most High God, do not torment me!"* **For He (Jesus) had been saying to him,** *"Come out of the man you unclean spirit!"* It would appear from the passage that Jesus was not having instant success with this deliverance. *And* then He was asking him, **"What is your name?"** We know that if Jesus had chosen to operate out of His divinity He would surely have known what He was dealing with and the name of the demon, but because He had chosen to limit himself he had to do some further inquiry. *"What is your name?"* Then the demon answers *"My name is legion for we are many."* Now Jesus knows what He is dealing with, so immediately He is able to successfully eradicate the demons from the man. Why this additional information made the difference in His success is a mystery. This is one example of how Jesus chose to limit Himself.

Also, in Luke 5:30-31 we read that as the crowds are pressing in on Jesus, a woman who had suffered twelve years with an issue of blood was forcing her way through the crowd. Having exhausted all her resources on the physicians of the day, she was desperate. However, she had faith, faith that if she could just touch the hem of Jesus' garment she would be healed. And when she did, she was instantly healed. What's interesting about this passage is that Jesus is instantly aware that power has gone out from Him, but He doesn't immediately know who touched Him. So, Jesus asks, **"Who is the one who touched Me?"** Had Jesus been operating out of His divinity he surely would have known who touched Him. This is another example that Jesus chose to limit Himself as a man dependent on the Holy Spirit.

Later, In Mark 9:18, 20-21, we read of a man desperate to see his son delivered from a cruel and tormenting spirit. This desperate father is explaining the symptoms of this demonization. *"Teacher, I brought You my son, possessed with a spirit that makes him mute: and whenever it seizes him, it dashes him to the ground and he foams at the mouth, and grinds his teeth, and stiffens out.........And they brought the boy to Him. And immediately the spirit threw him into a convulsion, and falling to the ground, he began rolling about and foaming at the mouth.* **And Jesus asked his father, 'How long has this been happening to him?'** *And he said, From his childhood."* Jesus then casts out the demon and the boy is healed and delivered. Again, we see Jesus is asking a question for more information. Jesus is deliberately choosing to not operate out of His divinity. Just so that I'm being clear, Jesus being fully God was also fully man. What I am asserting is that Jesus chose to operate throughout His earthly ministry as a man fully dependent on the Holy Spirit rather than choosing to operate out of His divinity.

Why did Jesus choose to do that? I believe He did that because if He had operated out of His divine side, then the supernatural gifts, miracles, healings prophecy, signs and wonders, would be regarded as unattainable. This would have left the church operating by its natural strength. But because Jesus operated as a man dependent on God, He left us a model to follow that we might access spiritual power and miracles through the Holy Spirit.

One night I was hanging out with a friend at school when we both saw a man that we both knew hobbling across the parking lot on crutches. He was taking a night course, and he had just been released from class. When we stopped to talk to him we noticed that in addition to the crutches, he was wearing what looked like a splint on his ankle. We asked what had happened and he explained to us that he had fallen off a platform and had landed on the side of his foot resulting in a severe injury. We then asked if we could pray for him. He said, "That would be great!" We were standing near his truck, so he sat on the bench seat sideways with the door open while we laid hands on his foot and began praying. As soon as we began praying I felt a surge of power or what felt like electricity going through my hand. He felt it as well, and before I could ask him to try out the foot, he began jumping around the parking lot saying, "I'm healed! I'm healed!"

We would never have experienced that if we had not taken the risk to step out and pray for that man's healing. Putting yourself in a position to be used of God in this capacity allows God to access your body to channel His love, grace and power to others.

REMOVING BLOCKS TO HEALING

There will be times when you pray for someone and they are not healed. Sometimes those reasons will remain a mystery. However, there are some fundamental reasons why some people are not healed. If you can identify that reason and resolve it, it can make a significant difference in the person's ability to receive their healing. We will discuss just a few of those reasons here.

- **Unconfessed Sin** – Sometimes people will come for prayer, and God wants to deal with something in that person's life. A person could be going to church and practicing sex with their boyfriend or girlfriend but acting like everything is hunky dory. In reality that is a sin and is blocking their healing. Always ask the Holy Spirit to show the person receiving prayer if there is anything He wants to show them. If the person reveals a sin, lead them through a prayer of forgiveness.
- **Unforgiveness** –In Matthew 6:14-15 Jesus said, *"If you forgive the sins of others when they sin against you, your sin will be forgiven. But if you do not forgive others their sins, then neither will your Father forgive your sins."* Once

in a while a person will be harboring bitterness or unforgiveness in their heart because of past hurts and deep wounding. This will often block a person from receiving any kind of healing. Ask if the person is aware of any- one they may need to forgive, and encourage them to forgive and release that person to God. Explain that forgiveness is not a feeling but a choice. Once they have forgiven the offender, go back to praying for the person's healing.

- **Unbelief** – Unbelief may block healing, but it is a very unpopular topic today because some have been made to feel condemned for their lack of faith by so called "Faith Healers." Set aside for a moment your denominational bias. Jesus talked a lot about unbelief. I have met people who have been in the church for years who are spiritually bankrupt in regards to faith. This is because of lack of experience, religious pride, or a faulty worldview based on rationalism or faulty teaching. Regardless of the reason, Jesus did say that faith would be required at some point. It could be the person praying or the person receiving prayer, but one thing is certain, someone has to have faith on one end or the other for healing to take place. One answer to this is to give the person a brief theology for healing by sharing some scripture verses on healing, and/or share some testimonies of others who have recently received healing or have been healed in the past. This is very effective for raising a person's faith level. Remember, Jesus said that all one needs is the faith of a mustard seed for healing to take place.
- **Faulty Teaching** – Sadly, some have been taught against healing by well-meaning church leaders.

These well-meaning teachers often give a rationalistic interpretation of the scriptures. Some either ignore certain scriptures or explain away the scriptures that are not easily understood. There is often a heavy emphasis on the historical gospel with very little of its current reality. Consequently, some people may have a theology and a belief system that does not allow them to believe God for healing. Try to identify the lie or faulty belief system, and then get the person receiving the prayer to renounce the faulty teaching or belief. Then get them to confess the truth of God's word. For example: *"By His stripes we are healed"*(I Peter 2:24).

- **Fear of Man** – The fear of what others may think about you or how you might look to others is called the "fear of man." The good news is that there is deliverance from this spirit that plagues most of mankind. Start out by renouncing it and resisting it. Then make a decision that you will not allow the spirit of the fear of man to dictate what you will and will not do for God.
- **Shame** – Shame is the most severe form of self-rejection. This self-rejection renders a person cut off and out of touch with the pain of their past. Often this is evident by a lack of emotional expression, flatness in affect or emotional numbness. This is a survival mechanism that allows a person to survive in an intolerable situation involving repeated trauma or abuse. Unfortunately, as an adult it can also act as a block to the healing of past hurts. One has to first deal with the shame before healing can happen. Ask the Holy Spirit to bring the person back to the point of trauma in their memory. Then get the person to forgive themselves for their vulnerability –allowing

themselves to be hurt or injured. This unforgiveness toward oneself is not rational, but it is real. You want them to reconcile with the part of themselves (often the child part) that was sinned against.

PREPARING FOR HEALING MINISTRY

My wife Lori and I lead group hikes now and then. Some of our groups have been substantially large numbering up to 15 or even 28 people. Some of these hikes have been anywhere between 10 to 22 miles round trip and very challenging. This means that our group would sometimes get very spread out, stretching even as much as a mile from the first person to the last. Feeling responsible, we were concerned about our friends getting lost or injured. So I bought a couple of rechargeable two-way radio handsets for communication. This worked fairly well in helping Lori and I keep track of everyone. She would often stay in front and I would bring up the rear to make sure we didn't lose any stragglers. The handsets allowed us to maintain communication between the front and the back of the group. It didn't take long for me to learn that I needed to leave the handsets in the charger the night before the hike. When I failed to do this once, I found out quickly that my wife and I lost power and communication because our batteries were low. This happened right in the middle of a major trek. It was getting late. Cell phones were not an option as there was no signal at the time. Not good.

Having fully charged batteries became critical for the longer treks if we were to maintain communication. It seems like a fairly basic and simple thing. When I set the handsets in the charger, the light would flash red indicating a low charge.

As the handset remained in the charger for a period of time, the light on the charger would eventually start to flash green indicating a full charge.

This comparison is relevant to healing ministry. We as human beings are just like the batteries in the handsets. Just like a battery is carbon-based, we also are carbon-based life forms. Consequently, we need to be charged before effective ministry can happen. God is the Charger. It's they that wait on the Lord that shall renew their strength, mount up on wings as eagles, run and not grow weary, walk and not faint (Isaiah 40:31). There is a supernatural increase that takes place both physically and spiritually when we marinate in God. Soak in prayer. Meditate on the word. Power increases as we "sit in the charger," or wait on God.

Jesus came as the Christ. Christ means "Anointed one." Anointed means: to be to be smudged, smeared or marked. Jesus came as one who was marked with the Holy Spirit. It was the anointing that Jesus sought to impart to His disciples. Jesus increased the anointing by spending time with the Father. This was his way of sitting in the charger, recharging His Spirit for the sustained periods of ministry that He, no doubt, knew would be necessary. Over and over again we see Jesus withdrawing to spend time with the Father. *"And He withdrew from there in a boat, to a lonely spot by Himself"* (Matthew 14:13). *"After He sent the crowds away, He went up to a mountain by Himself to pray; and when it was evening, He was there alone"* (Matthew 14:23). *"And when day came, He departed and went to a lonely place"* (Luke 4:42).

When we receive the Holy Spirit, we receive a taste of that same anointing that Jesus had. It is God's Spirit that uses us to heal and to do miracles. That's why it is critically important to cultivate God's anointing on our lives. As a rechargeable battery is recharged with power by the electric current going through the charger, so it is in like manner that the believer receives and increases spiritual power by remaining in the presence of God. This relationship is facilitated through time alone, solitude and silence, meditating on scripture, personal worship, waiting in His presence, or what I like to call soaking. The more a believer soaks in God's presence the more they are recharged with spiritual power.

We see that Moses also increased in power and radiance the more time he spent in God's presence. So much so that people could actually see the glory of God (the anointing) on him (Exodus 34:29). This anointing or radiance was something that was evident and could be seen.

However, Moses kept his face covered because he knew that the Glory of God's radiance on him faded over time. So he would cover himself until he could return to God's manifest presence and "recharge" (Exodus 34:29-35).

The same is true for us as believers. The more time we spend with God, the more of God that rubs off on us. Then we carry that residue into our ministry time. The increase of God's anointing on us will often mean more effective ministry happening with healing, miracles, signs and wonders. Our spirit is charged by His presence and we are refreshed, empowered, and equipped to do the works of God. Time with God is essential if you are going to be optimally effective in ministry.

HEALING GUIDELINES

When you practice healing there are just a few things that become necessary as well as pragmatic. First of all, keep your eyes open. Most of us have been drilled in the practice of closing our eyes when praying for others. I believe this practice started out of reverence for God, or perhaps some were ashamed to be seen praying, so everyone just agreed not to watch each other. Whatever the reason, It's not a very good practice for healing ministry. You cannot see what the Spirit of God is doing with a person when your eyes are closed. To discern what the Holy Spirit is doing with someone, it helps to watch them through the process.

Also, ask permission before you lay hands on others. Some who ask for healing prayer have been subject to sexual or physical abuse, and your touch could be misinterpreted. It is estimated that one out of four people has been the victim of sexual abuse or some form of molestation. Be sensitive to anyone who comes to you for healing prayer.

Another thing that needs mentioning is that you need to give yourself the freedom to fail. The first person that I tried to minister healing to died right in front of me on their deathbed. I'm glad to say that this doesn't happen often. I could have allowed discouragement to keep me from pursuing healing ministry, but I kept praying for people and God eventually gave me breakthrough. Be persistent and don't give up. God wants to heal, but He also wants people who will believe Him for it.

Most importantly, give God's love to those you minister to. As I said before in Chapter 3, Love, Love, Love. If no apparent healing is happening, that person should still walk away having received God's love through us. This is the golden rule of healing prayer. Give God's love first, and then give God's love last.

A BASIC PROCESS TO HEALING PRAYER

- **Prayer Topic**- The first thing I do in healing ministry is to ask the person what they want prayer for. What they say may or may not be the real problem. Listen to them as you are also listening to the Holy Spirit.

- **Root Problem** - Ask the Holy Spirit to help you find out the root cause of the person's issue or malady. Again, they may or may not know what the root is. Some diseases, for example, have their root in bitterness and unforgiveness. Be gentle in your questioning. Keep listening to the Holy Spirit. It is the root issue that you want to pray for and minister healing to.

- **Ministry Need** – Once you have identified the root issue, you can then decide what kind of ministry the person needs. Ask the Lord how He wants you to pray, and wait on Him. There is no reason to rush into the ministry phase unless you know how God wants you to pray. It may be for physical healing, or it may be for a more internal/emotional issue such as self-rejection, fear, unforgiveness, addiction, abuse, or it may be a demonic problem. Unless you know, wait, wait wait.

- **Ministry Application** – As you begin praying, keep looking for what the Holy Spirit may be doing. There may be a deep peace that comes on a person; there may be tears, crying or even sobbing, Laughter, joy or a change in countenance may occur. Be listening for what direction God wants to go in. The Holy Spirit will lead the session. Be sensitive, look and listen. You will know when there is breakthrough of some kind. You will know that ministry is over when you either sense it's over or when God tells you it's over.

- **After Care** – Once ministry is over, emphasize God's love for the person regardless of what healing has taken place. Focus on what God has done, not on what He hasn't. Offer future prayer follow-up. Offer general guidance and encouragement; make referrals to small group involvement, fellowship, scripture reading, and living in holiness and obedience to God.
- **Cover and Seal Ministry Session** - After ministering to a person, pray a covering over them sealing what the Holy Spirit has done. Pray the blood of Jesus and protection over the person, sealing what God has done. This is to prevent counter attack and the stealing of anything God has done in that person.

I hope that you can understand and appreciate the benefits of being equipped for healing prayer ministry within the grand scale of this spiritual war that is, in fact, part of our physical and spiritual reality. Healing prayer is one of the primary weapons for destroying the works of the devil. Part of this healing ministry involves delivering people from demonic bondage. In the following chapter we will look at deliverance as another spiritual weapon of warfare, a weapon that every believer should have at least a working knowledge of.

Next we will look at some basic principles to help believers be better prepared to minster to the demonized.

CHAPTER 12

DELIVERANCE MINISTRY

"When a strong man, fully armed, guards his own
house, his possessions are undisturbed. But when
someone stronger than he attacks and overpowers
him, he takes away from him all his armor on which
he has relied and distributes his plunder."
Luke 11:21-22 NASB

I was serving at a church in Southern California to fulfill my pastoral internship requirements at the time I met him. Luis (not his real name) was a recovering drug addict, and at the time, was homeless. The church had provided a place for Luis to stay as they were helping him to stay off drugs and get on his feet. He had been complaining about some strange things going on at the place he was staying. He seemed a little freaked. He told me that he was not sleeping much and that he was tired all the time. When I inquired further about what the problem was, he began to describe things I was not expecting. I didn't know if he was imagining what he was describing or if he was still doing drugs and was possibly hallucinating. I had very little experience with the demonic at the time, but thought there could be more to his story so I listened intently. He went on to explain that he was hearing things at night, and that "things" were waking him up when he would try to sleep. I asked Luis if I could pray for him and he agreed, so I put my hand on his shoulder. As I began to pray, Luis's face began to wince as he complained about a knot forming in his lower back. He said it felt like an extreme Charlie horse. The pain was bad. So I moved my hand to where he said the knot was, and I continued to pray. As I did so, I watched as the knot moved up his back, to his shoulder and left him. I had never experienced anything like it. It was then that I suspected that there might be more to his nightly disturbances.

I was staying with Luis for a time while the church was seeking to make other living arrangements for me. It had been previously arranged that I was to house sit for a couple while they were out of town. Since they had not yet started their vacation, I was asked to stay with Luis, something I was very willing to do. I really had no idea what I was getting into, but lacking another place to stay for the summer, I wasn't about to be picky. Besides, I was morbidly curious as well.

The first night started out as a fairly uneventful and normal evening, but as Luis and I sought to get some well-needed shut eye, things started happening. I have never experienced anything like it, nor have I since. That night was followed by a number of strange phenomena. Throughout the night we were awakened by loud knocks on the bedroom door, although there was no one else in our dwelling (I confirmed that myself). We heard repeated tapping on the ceiling and walls, the sound of footsteps in the hallway (like someone wearing dress shoes on linoleum) and again there was no one there. We even turned lights on and walked throughout the rooms to confirm that no one else was there. We also later heard once an audible growl coming from the ceiling. This didn't sound like an animal growl. No, it sounded more human than that. We immediately looked at each other to confirm that we both heard the same thing. Each time I would rebuke these entities in the name of Jesus, commanding them to stop and go away, and each time it was to no avail.

Fear gripped us, and the harassment continued throughout the night. As a Christian I knew Jesus was greater in power and authority. I knew demons had to bow to Jesus' name. Yet, my rebukes and commands were ignored, as though I were being laughed at by these unseen tormentors. Here I was, an intern pastor, and I was completely ineffective at doing anything about this situation. What I didn't know at that time was that I too had inroads in my own life from my past that were, at the time, still unresolved. Although I had received Christ, there were still in my past unbroken agreements that I had made with the enemy, soul ties that were still, at that time, unbroken. This gave the demonic access and grounds for harassment. I knew nothing of such things at the time. I had entered into a battle without knowing what the rules were. My ignorance had given place to the enemy, and I was at a loss to know what to do. These laws I would later come to understand. Needless to say, we didn't get a lot of sleep that night. That experience motivated me to get to a place where I would understand these spiritual "laws" or "rules" that later allowed me to defeat the enemy in my own life, and later still in the lives of others.

GOVERNING LAWS OF THE SPIRIT REALM

In the beginning of this book I shared with you Wendy's story of deliverance and how she was set free from tormenting spirits. Wendy had gateways or portals opened up to the demonic early in her life. These portals had to be closed before Wendy could be set free. In chapter two, I talked about the "rules of engagement" regarding spiritual warfare. Most people are unaware of these spiritual laws that govern the spirit realm. Even believers can be unaware of these laws, some even choosing to remain willfully ignorant to the spiritual realities that shape the lives and destinies of so many. Here I want to emphasize a spiritual law that's been a theme throughout this book. This law has to do with spiritual rights. The law that bears repeating is *that the demonic needs permission to do anything. He is not allowed access to the believer who walks in obedience to God. Therefore, the enemy can only gain access to a person through sin and disobedience to God. This can be sin we commit or sin committed against us by another. These sins can be access points or what some call doorways or portals. These portals can give the demonic access or rights to a person.*

When a person sins they give access, rights or grounds for the demonic to attack, afflict, harass, torment or even possess them. When a person is subject to the demonic, they are to one degree or another influenced by these entities. Demons are malevolent spirits, so they seek to destroy the very host they have influence over. This can be in the form of harmful thoughts or words, various addictions, suicide, and numerous acts of violence.

Deliverance is simply denying access to the demon(s). Deliverance is done easily by closing these portals or access points and by taking the enemy's rights away from him. The demonic has six distinct gateways or portals to gain access to a person. It's the number of access points that are open in a person's life that often determine the severity of demonization or the degree of influence demons can exert over an individual. I will define these six entry points that I will call portals, and give the steps to closing them.

DELIVERANCE 101

SIX PORTALS OF DEMONIZATION

Portal # 1. - Fear and Trauma

Fear and trauma can serve as a gateway for demonic bondage. One time a woman came into the courthouse when I was on my break at work. She appeared to be in her early seventies. I was walking down the hallway when I saw her. She was literally shaking. Her fear was obvious. She had come for some legal matter, and she was crying and breathing hard. I had seen this kind of fear only a few times in ministry. I stopped and asked her if she was ok. She tried to ask me for directions and was so afraid that she even had difficulty thinking straight or communicating. I pulled her aside to get her out of the flow of the pedestrian traffic, and asked if I could pray for her. She said that I could, so I put my hand on her shoulder and began to pray. I spoke softly, praying the blood of Jesus over her. I gently took authority over the spirit of fear saying, *"I come against the spirit of fear, and in the name of Jesus, I command the spirit of fear to cease and desist in the name of Jesus. I release Your peace, Holy Spirit, over this woman, and I invite You to minister to her heart and mind. Cover and protect her in Jesus name -Amen."* As I prayed, she began to calm down, and I could see that peace was beginning to return to her. Her heavy breathing and her tears began to subside, and she began to return to her right mind. She was able to think and communicate clearly again. As she began to settle she asked if there was a place where she could sit down, so I directed her to some chairs. She went and sat down as the Holy Spirit continued to minister to her, the fear having relented.

A spirit of fear can manifest in different ways, but is typically characterized by fear that is often irrational. Some refer to it as the dark night of the soul. It can come in the form of panic attacks, night terrors, nightmares, a constant nervousness, or an overall sense of impending doom, a dark cloud, or like the other shoe is about to drop any minute. It is important to recognize that fear was never intended to be man's natural state when God created him. Fear came after the fall of mankind and is a spirit that seeks to oppress, limit, and restrict mankind's potential. People who have given place to a spirit of fear typically refuse to take risks. As the spirit of fear is given place in a person's life, it grows more oppressive over time, restricting more and more of that person's life. Playing it safe becomes the primary default setting in a person's decision-making process.

A fortress of fear is built and is established over time. A spirit of fear is given place through negative assumptions and is, in turn, built by negative words. Fear is based on a negative belief system. This system is built on negative assumptions which are built by negative words and /or experiences typically when we are very young. A spirit of fear is usually given place in a fear-based family system. A child growing up in a fear based-family system will often receive threats such as, *"Come here now or I will beat you within an inch of your life!"* Curses may be uttered such as, *"You will never amount to anything!"* *"You're stupid!"* and negative assumptions such as, *"I don't want you to riding your bike; you're going to get hit by a car!"* Negative assumptions presume the worst of any situation. It's a "glass half empty" mentality.

It's the negative words and assumptions in fear-based families that undermine a child's sense of value, self-worth and identity. This lack of value and identity diminishes security and confidence. This undermining of a person's sense of value and identity through words leaves a void in a person's life that gives a place for fear to reside. Over time this becomes a fortress of fear in the person's life. In a healthy family system children are given love, nurture, positive affirmations and words that serve to build self-worth and value. Children growing up with these positive words have a strong sense of identity and who they are. Positive messages and affirmations help children to feel confident and secure, allowing them to take reasonable risks in life. This leaves little, if any, place for fear to reside or take root. The spirit of fear, on the other hand, finds a place to dwell in a person (human host) through agreement with negative assumptions (i.e. lies). With these negative assumptions children grow up learning to believe the worst. This gives the spirit of fear fertile ground to grow in.

DISMANTLING THE FORTRESS OF FEAR

It's important that we understand that we empower the spirit of fear through our agreement with these lies (false or negative assumptions). As we grow up believing these lies, a fortress of fear is built and eventually established in our life. Fear is putting your faith in circumstances rather than God. We are delivered from the spirit of fear when we begin to take steps to dismantle fear's fortress.

- Deliverance from the spirit of fear begins to happen the minute we make a decision of our will to break agreement with the enemy. This involves identifying these lies, false assumptions, and negative belief systems.
- Discover the origin of these lies or false beliefs. (This may require healing, depending on the severity

of these past hurts or trauma. Invite Jesus into the memory at the point of trauma. Forgiveness of those who have hurt us may be necessary.)

- Say, *"I break my agreement with the spirit of fear, and all fear's lies in Jesus' name!"*
- Renounce each of the lies, negative beliefs, and false assumptions. Renounce any inner vows made based on these lies.
- Declare and decree God's truth in place of these lies.
- Finally, renounce the spirit of fear.
- Command the spirit of fear to leave, never to return. Say, *"I renounce the spirit of fear! You have no place in my life! I take authority over fear, and I command it to leave, never to return in Jesus' name!"*

Portal # 2. - Bitterness & Unforgiveness

Unforgiveness can also give the demons a gateway that can lead to bitterness. It is well known that bitterness is often the root cause of cancer and a whole host of various other maladies. Proverbs 14:30 says, *"A tranquil heart is life to the body, but passion is rottenness to the bones."* The word "passion" denotes a strong or intense emotion. Bitterness certainly qualifies as an intense emotion, and the scripture indicates that this can have a negative impact on a person's physical health. Smith Wigglesworth, a well-known healing evangelist of the late 1800's and the early 1900's, made a strong assertion that cancer was actually a spirit, and that the spirit of cancer actually needed to be eradicated from an afflicted person's body. It stands to reason, then, that over time unforgiveness can give place to bitterness, and later to a number of afflicting maladies. That's why Ephesians 4:26 encourages us to keep short accounts with people that cause us offense. *"...do not let the sun go down on your anger, and do not give the devil an opportunity."* Disease, affliction, and demonic bondage almost always have a core of unforgiveness that needs to be addressed if the person is to be delivered and set free. Deliverance closes the portal of bitterness and unforgiveness and begins by getting a person to forgive those who have hurt, wounded and sinned against them. I often explain that forgiveness is not a feeling but a decision of the will. Jesus said, *"For if you forgive men when they sin against you, your heavenly Father will also forgive you. But if you do not forgive men their sins, your heavenly Father will not forgive your sins."* Matthew 6:14-15 Unforgiveness leaves a person open and vulnerable to spiritual attack.

Start by asking the Holy Spirit to show the person seeking deliverance who they need to forgive. Sometimes they know right away who it is they need to forgive. Other times they are not consciously aware that they are angry with anyone. Wait on God. As God begins to show them who they need to forgive, I like to lead them through a prayer that sounds something like this:

PRAYER OF FORGIVENESS

"Father God I lift up (name the person) to You, and in the name of Jesus I choose to forgive them.

I choose to forgive them for..... (Have them state the offense, violation, sin. This is important because they need to be consciously aware of what they are giving over and releasing to God)

I release their debt to me, and I give it to You Lord. I ask You to cover (name the person) sin with the blood of Jesus, and I ask You Father to bless them in Jesus' name.

Forgive me for my unforgiveness and cover my sin in the blood of Jesus.

Thank You, Father, for setting me free. - Amen"

Once the person has forgiven everyone they are aware of needing to forgive, take authority over the demon in that person's life. I'll say something like, *"I take authority over this spirit, and I command this afflicting and harassing spirit to leave this person now, never to return - in Jesus Name!* Ask the person how they are doing. Get some feedback. This will help you assess what's going on. Often you can see a visible release on a person's face, a visible change in their countenance.

Portal # 3. - Pornography

Demonization is often linked to pornography. Pornography is a big problem in the Westernized nations of the world, and though it is thought of by many to be an innocuous pastime, it is, a serious portal to the demonic. It is well known that a large number of people struggle with some form of sexual addiction. Much of the reason for this is demonic bondage that has come through pornography. Many think of pornography as harmless, but nothing could be further from the truth. It is true that the eyes are the window to the soul. Jesus said, that the eyes are the lamp of the body, and if our eyes are clear our whole body is full of light, but if our eyes are bad, our whole body is full of darkness. (Matthew 6:22-23) Jesus was referring to a spiritual darkness that comes over a person whose eyes continually gravitate toward the forbidden. Our eyes can become a portal to demonic bondage. The pornography industry is a multi-billion dollar industry. Demonic bondage resulting from pornography continues to destroy countless marriages, families and individual lives. It is even documented that a number of occultic organizations are closely linked and even funded by the pornography industry. Small wonder why it is a growing problem in the world today!

A man I will call Mike (not his real name), was in his early thirties when he came for help. He explained that he was newly engaged to a woman he had been dating for some time, and they were planning to get married soon. As I listened, Mike proceeded to confess that he was struggling with lust for other women. He said that he had never cheated on his fiancée, but was concerned that he could jeopardize his relationship. As I probed a little further, I learned that Mike had been into pornography and was still perusing the magazines on a regular basis. He went on to share that he was experiencing involuntary sexual arousal at night and often had difficulty sleeping. I asked him if he had been intimate with any other women in his past. He said that, in fact, there had been a number of other women before meeting his fiancée. It became apparent to me that the pornography, together with the illicit sex with these other women in Mike's past, had opened a gateway that allowed the demonic to gain access in his life. This foothold caused Mike to feel unable to break the cycle of lust that seemed to overwhelm him at times.

When I had enough information, we started Mike's deliverance. First, I led Mike through a prayer of confession that went something like this:

- *Father God, I confess my sins of pornography and lust, fornication, adultery and idolatry; I confess all this activity as sin. I know and acknowledge that this activity is wrong in Your sight and displeasing to You.*
- *Father, in the name of Jesus, I renounce these sins of pornography and lust, fornication, adultery and idolatry.*

I then had Mike write down the first names of all the women he remembered having sex with. Afterwards, I took him down the list of each woman, breaking all soul ties between him and each woman on the list. Note: (When breaking soul ties, be careful to **only** break the **ungodly** soul ties) I will say more about soul ties later.

- *Father God, I lift up (name the person) to You, and in the name of Jesus Christ, I break and sever all (ungodly) soul ties between me and (name the person). Everything that has been transferred to (him/her) from me, I take back in Jesus' name, and everything that has been transferred to me from (him/her) I give back in Jesus' name. Forgive the sin, and heal the damage created by this ungodly union and seal your work in Jesus' name.*

I then had Mike break all soul ties with the spirit of pornography and lust. This proved to be a necessary and profound step because over time a relationship is developed between the demon and the host. The person is held in bondage through the pleasure and gratification of pornography, masturbation, and illicit sex. As I told Mike that he needed to break all soul ties with the spirit of pornography and lust, I could see him really struggling. I knew that he wasn't taking this decision lightly. Mike knew very well that he needed to do this, and so he prayed. As Mike began to pray, he struggled to repeat the prayer out loud. He even had difficulty forming the words because the bondage was so strong. Mike eventually spoke the following prayer out loud and, as he did, he broke down sobbing.

- *Father God, I lift up my addiction to the spirit of pornography and lust to You, and in the name of Jesus, I break and sever all soul ties between me and the spirit of pornography. I break and sever all soul ties between me and the spirit of lust. Any pleasure or benefit I received from these spirits I renounce in Jesus' name. Anything that has been transferred to me from pornography or lust I renounce and command to go in Jesus' name!*

The Holy Spirit brought Mike to a place of deep repentance and was setting him free. Next I had Mike pray, asking the Father to forgive and cover all his sins in the blood of Jesus.

- *Father God, I repent of all my participation in pornography and lust, and I ask You to forgive me for these sins. I ask You, Lord, to cover all these sins in the blood of Jesus. Cleanse, wash and purge me from all sin. Thank You for Your forgiveness Father, in Jesus' name - Amen.*

Next, I took authority over the spirit of pornography, lust and idolatry. I said:

- *"I take authority over the spirits of pornography, lust and idolatry, and I command you to go - in Jesus' name! You no longer have any right to be here - Go now, and don't come back - in Jesus' name!"*

Finally, I asked Father God to fill Mike with the Holy Spirit and to seal his work. Sometimes, if I think it's necessary, I petition God to send warring angels to sweep the temple (of the person's body) clean.

- *Father, fill him now with Your Holy Spirit, fill and overflow him now Lord. Send Your warring angels to sweep Your*

> *temple clean, and seal the work You have done with the blood of Jesus – Amen.*

God brought about a powerful deliverance, and I am happy to say that Mike was set free that day. Hallelujah! God's power and grace continue to set lives free!

Portal # 4. – Illicit Sex

She was seventeen years old when she came seeking help. Her name was Dawn (not her real name). At the time she came for ministry, I could see a visible heaviness on her. She appeared very somber and depressed. When I asked her why she wanted prayer, she said that she was very unhappy and was struggling with feeling depressed all the time. I asked if she was a believer and she said that she was. As I talked to Dawn a little more, she confessed to having sex with her boyfriend even though they were not married. When I questioned if she had had sex with anyone else prior to her current relationship, she sheepishly admitted having many different partners over the last three years. She shared that in the past she had always been a happy person, but that over the last year or so, she was getting more and more depressed.

I asked her if she understood that sex outside a covenant of marriage was a sin against God, and she said she did. I explained that sexual sin gives the enemy grounds or rights to oppress you. I said that God's word teaches that when a man and a woman come together in sexual union that the two become one flesh, which means that their souls become tied and knitted together. I went on to explain to her that when a person has sex with a number of different people, that person can pick up all the spiritual "baggage" that each of those individuals have, and that there may be a transferring of spirits. So, for example, if a person has dabbled in pornography or the occult, and they pick up demons associated with those activities, you can open a gateway by having sex with that person, allowing those spirits access to your life as well. The result can be severe oppression. So if a person has several demons, any or all those spirits can transfer to anyone else that person has sex with. The ramifications of multiple sex partners can have a cumulative effect on a person as that person acquires a number of different bad or unclean spirits. This often manifests in severe oppression, depression, addiction, or even physical maladies. Once I explained the serious ramifications of casual sex, I had Dawn's full attention.

I asked Dawn if she understood all that I said, and she said she did. I then explained to her that if she wanted help, and if she truly wanted to be set free, she would need to embrace true repentance which would mean abstaining from sex with her boyfriend until they were married. I explained that it would also mean severing all soul ties with any boys she had had sex with in her past. I asked her if she were willing to do that. I could see that Dawn was thinking about it and taking it all in. After a short reflection, she agreed to repent of her sin. So, I had her make a list of all the boys she had sex with. Once she wrote down every name she could think of, we then started down the list breaking and severing all soul ties between Dawn and the boys in these ungodly unions. I had Dawn repeat the following prayer:

- *Father God, I lift up (name the person) to you. And in the name of Jesus Christ, I break and sever all (ungodly) soul ties between me and (name the person) in Jesus' name. Everything that has been transferred to him from me I take back in Jesus' name, and everything that transferred to me from him, I give back in Jesus' name. Forgive my sin, and heal the damage created by this ungodly union and seal your work in Jesus' name – Amen.*

Once we went through the list of names. I led Dawn through a simple prayer of repentance:

- *Father God, I acknowledge my sin against you by practicing sex outside your intended purpose, a covenant of marriage. I'm sorry Father, and I ask you to forgive all my sins and cover them with the blood of Jesus. I ask You, Father, to cleanse, wash, and purge me from all defilement in Jesus' name –Amen.*

I then pronounced Dawn forgiven in the name of Jesus.

- *Father God, as Christ's representative and as Dawn's brother in Jesus, I pronounce her forgiven in Jesus' name, and I declare her the righteousness of God. Fill her now with Your Holy Spirit.*
- *Thank You, Lord, for Your forgiveness and blessing. In Jesus' name. Amen!*

By the end of our prayer, God had lifted all that oppression off Dawn. Her countenance was completely changed, and she was beaming. She then commented saying, *"I feel so light!"* Jesus Christ had once again set another captive free.

Portal # 5. Drugs and Alcohol

When I was a student, I was on my way to a short term mission trip to Mexico with a college group. We were going to

Tecate to help oversee groups of high school students. These students were to help build homes for those who lived near a dump. We were operating through the local church there and building homes for families the local pastor wanted to help. We were on our way there from Orange County and had gotten a late start. It was nighttime when we finally got over the border. As we were on the road to Tecate, I remember something our driver (also our team leader) said that really stuck with me, "Pray that God protects us from any drunks on the road. Demons will blackout drivers under the influence and will try to run their vehicles into ours." He also mentioned that it had happened before, which raised my concerns.

I remember having one of those "aha" moments thinking, *"Wow, people under the influence of drugs or alcohol are often under the influence of demons as well."* I remember it becoming apparent to me that when a person blacks out, it is essentially the demon taking over this human vehicle (host). At that point the demon is literally in the driver's seat. I remember hearing of people driving home after a night of heavy drinking and never knowing or remembering how they got home. I remember hearing how those under the influence of drugs and alcohol often steer their cars into the lights of police vehicles stopped on the side of the road. Knowing the enemy's agenda, I began to think of all the accidents, injury, fights, rapes and shootings that involved alcohol or drugs. In a moment, it became crystal clear to me that any person using mind-altering substances to get high not only lowers their inhibitions, but also opens a portal for demonic occupation and influence.

Demonization through drugs and alcohol lead many into addiction, bondage, and multiple vices brought on largely by the influence of demonic powers. This can often originate from a single act of rebellion that opens a portal to demonic bondage. *"Rebellion is as the sin of witchcraft, and insubordination is as iniquity and idolatry"* (1Samuel 15:23). I remember a testimony of a man coming to get prayer. He had a bad addiction to cigarettes. Time and time again he had tried to quit but had continually failed. When he was asked to remember when his smoking started, he began to recollect a time when he was a teenager. He said that he was very angry with his parents at the time, and remembered sneaking out at night to smoke a cigarette against their wishes. He said he had been smoking ever since. It was this single act of rebellion that was the portal by which a spirit of addiction was able to get a hold on his life. Once the origin was understood, he was directed to renounce his rebellion against his parents. Once he renounced and repented of this rebellion, he was set free from cigarettes for the first time since he had started smoking.

It has been true for centuries that mind-altering drugs of various kinds have been used in different forms of pagan ritual and demon worship, including witchcraft and sorcery. It is the drug that opens a person's mind and soul to spirit entities that influence them toward acts of sin and self-destruction that give the enemy even more rights to further torment the individual.

DELIVERANCE FROM THE
SPIRIT OF ADDICTION

Deliverance from drugs and alcohol requires the true will and desire to be free. As with other addictions, there is a relationship formed between the addictive spirit and the person. This is a relationship that needs to be broken.

So the first thing I ask a person who comes for help is, do you truly want to be set free? If what they are seeking through ministry is merely temporary relief from some immediate circumstance, that just will not do. There must be a commitment to repentance and long-term freedom. Also, social networks are developed though drug use which may not necessarily be healthy or beneficial. Healthy support systems need to be put in place for follow-up of the person desiring to be free once and for all. This should be explained to them. Assuming they truly want to be set free and are committed to making different choices. I would take them through the following process for deliverance:

Have the person make the following declarations.

- *Father God, I declare that I want to be completely free from all addiction to drugs and alcohol in Jesus' name. I recognize that I am powerless in and of myself to get free, and I call on the power of Your grace to set me free.*
- *I confess my addiction to drugs and alcohol, and I renounce any lie that I am an addict. Rather, I declare the truth that I am the righteousness of God in Christ Jesus. I renounce, repent and turn away from my addictive and self-willed lifestyle. I renounce the spirit of addiction. I renounce the spirit of idolatry. I choose to embrace and pursue my new identity in Christ.*
- *I renounce my rebellion against You, Lord, or my family members. I renounce any and all occultic practices that I have committed in ignorance. I renounce any and all participation in witchcraft.*
- *Father God, I choose to forgive (Name the person or persons who have hurt you or sinned against you in any way) for*

(causing me pain, rejection, abandonment, abuse, etc.). I release their debt to me and I give it to You, Lord, and I ask you to bless them in Jesus' name.

- *Father, forgive my sins as I have forgiven those who have hurt and sinned against me. I ask You, Father, to cover all my sins in the blood of Jesus. Cleanse me from all defilement of the spirit, soul, and body in Jesus' name.*

- *I renounce all lies, vows, and agreements that I have made with the enemy. (Name specific lies, vows, agreements and false beliefs) and I break any and all agreements (name specific agreements) with the enemy, and I confess the truth (declare God's word of truth in place of the lie).*

- Next, break and sever any and all ungodly soul ties with addicted parents and/or others where there has been an ungodly sexual union. *Say, Father God, I lift up my (father, mother, sexual partner) and in the name of Jesus, I break and sever all ungodly soul ties from (him/ her) to me and from me to (him /her) in Jesus' name. All that has transferred to me I give back in Jesus' name and all that transferred from me to (him/her) I take back, in Jesus' name.*

- Then break the bloodline of alcoholism from parents where addiction has been evident in the family line. *Say: Father God, I lift my father/ mother up to you, and in the name of Jesus Christ I break and sever the bloodline of drugs/alcohol from my father/ mother to me and from me to my father/mother back to the first, second, third and fourth generations in Jesus' name - Amen.*

- Take authority over the spirit of addiction say: *I take authority over the spirit of addiction and in the name of Jesus I command you to leave now, never to return! Go!*

- I then petition Father God to send in His holy angels to sweep His temple clean. Ask Him to expose anything that doesn't belong there. *Father bring Your light into all the dark places and dispel all darkness.*

- Next pray for protection and the infilling of the Holy Spirit. Say: *Father God, I ask you to seal all that You have done today in the blood of Jesus. I pray a hedge of protection over_____. Surround them with Your holy angels, in Jesus' name. Amen.*

Deliverance can be a lengthy process at times, but once you have taken away the demon's rights to be there, they have to go. The enemy no longer has any grounds to justify his occupation. He has to go! Stand on the truth and stand your ground, Christian! The last portal of entry we will look at is the occult.

Portal # 6 The Occult

Beazy (not his real name) was a loner and extremely wounded and angry at God. Between the ages of six and ten, within a four year span of time, Beazy lost his dad to cancer. Also, his mother was sick and suffering health problems that required surgery. During this time Beazy was also being repeatedly molested by his babysitter. Later, his brother was also diagnosed with cancer. This stream of events began to fuel a rage and an anger that he chose to direct toward God. For escape, Beazy began listening to satanic rock music. His emotion, pain, fear and desperate need for attention caused him to express his anger through the satanic music. In his pain he felt a need to place blame, and he placed that blame on Jesus. As Beazy got older, he more and more embraced a satanic persona.

Beazy lost hope, feeling there was no real meaning to life. At this point Beazy didn't care about anything. His persona began to intimidate people around him, and he discovered that this gave him a sense of power and control. His hate and anger kept him from feeling vulnerable. Over time, Beazy started to have demonic dreams that would wake him up at night. At one point he even started to see red eyes looking at him when he knew he was fully awake. Later, he began to mock Christians.

One day Beazy noticed a married couple walking around his street praying over the houses and the neighborhood. Time and time again, the couple would come around. Beazy eventually met them and discovered they were Christians. Over time a relationship developed. After some time, he began to meet other Christians. Beazy was being impacted on a profound level as these believers continued to love and embrace him. Over the course of time Beazy started attending the church services. One Sunday as the pastor gave an invitation, Beazy got up to leave when this strong sense came to him that he needed to turn around and go to the altar, or something bad was going to happen. It was as though God Himself was giving Beazy a warning, if not an ultimatum. Beazy turned and went to the altar. As he knelt and started praying, he started to see a vision of all these demons trying to come after him, but he could also see a bubble around him, protecting him from harm. Then out of nowhere, a voice told him to slit the pastor's throat! Beazy said that he noticed a number of people interceding for him. All of a sudden, Beazy was filled with anxiety and rage! In his own words, *"I wanted to kill the pastor, and I wanted to kill the intercessors, so I went after one of the women. Three men tackled me and held me back. I thought, I am not bowing to Jesus! I started spitting and cursing and trying to kill someone! As the men held me down, they and several women who were intercessors, started to pray, casting demons out of me. I did receive Jesus Christ that night, and eventually I was delivered from an antichrist spirit. Afterward, I felt a sense of peace I had not felt before. Throughout that year I had several different prayer teams pray for me, and eventually I was completely free. "*

I would like to point out that Beazy technically never really got deep into occultic practices. His demonization came out of expressed and intentional agreement with the demonic and anger toward God.

TV shows and movies like Bewitched and Harry Potter have served to romanticize the occult, painting a picture of black magic as innocent, fun, and even playful at times. With the onset of post-Christianity in America, we have seen a virtual explosion of interest in the occult. New Age, Eastern mysticism, witchcraft, and Satanism all have sought to answer the cry of a generation seeking something real, something experiential, not realizing or understanding the danger involved in these practices. As a result, more and more people have become enslaved to the demonic. This kind of bondage can manifest itself in a number of ways. The torment associated with a person desiring to escape occultic ties can be a challenging road as the enemy fights to keep claim of its host.

The Bible is very clear that God forbids dabbling in or practicing any aspect of the occult. In Leviticus 19 God commands His people saying, *"Do not practice divination or sorcery.... "Do not turn to mediums or seek out spiritists, for you will be defiled by them. I am the Lord your God."* and in Deuteronomy 18:10- 12 we read: *"There shall not be found among you anyone who makes his son or daughter pass through the fire, one who uses divination, one who practices witchcraft, or one who interprets omens, or a sorcerer, or one who casts a spell, or a medium, or a spiritists, or one who calls up the dead. For whoever does these things is detestable to the Lord..."*

God makes it abundantly clear in His word that to violate His commands will cause those who do so to be defiled. The word "defile" means to be made unclean, impure or contaminated. It is this defilement that gives the enemy rights or grounds to oppress a person. Any occultic practice whatsoever may open a portal to demonic tormentors or oppression.

There is great news, however! It's the Blood of Jesus Christ that can cleanse a person from all defilement. The power of Christ's resurrection can reverse a person's status before God. When a person's sin is forgiven and they are covered in the Blood of Jesus, the devil has no more rights to that person! So now the person stands holy and blameless!

Some Christians believe that once a person accepts Jesus Christ, no demons can continue to torment them. In most cases this is true. However, when a person has made agreements or contracts with the demonic (whether verbal or written) these agreements still stand until the believer breaks and renounces them. So when a person who has been involved in the occult receives Christ, the war is won; however, the battle is often just beginning. The enemy's power over that person is broken. Now, it's just a matter of identifying past agreements made with the enemy, breaking and renouncing them. At the point at which all agreements have been broken, the demons have to leave. They have no rights. They have no grounds. They must go!

Casting out Demons

Here is a simple model prayer I like to use when I want to help someone get free from demons. Let me also stress the importance of bringing to any deliverance session a vital connection with God, for it is He who provides us with the anointing and power to set the captives free.

- First, identify any of the six portals that may be open. Take the person through the list of possibilities: Fear, Unforgiveness, Pornography, Illicit Sex, Drugs/ Alcohol, The Occult. Write them down if there is more than one.
- If the person is not a Christian, first lead them through a prayer of salvation. If they are a Christian, have them identify, confess and pray a prayer of repentance for their sin. Make sure specific sins are mentioned and covered in the blood. Say: *"Father, I confess my sins of (mention specific sins). I know these sins have been displeasing to You and have broken our relationship. I am sorry for displeasing You. Help me to truly repent by Your grace and cover my sin in the Blood of Jesus."*
- Then have the person forgive any and all persons who have hurt or offended them. Lead them through a prayer of forgiveness. Say: *"Father God, I lift up (name the person) to You. And in the name of Jesus Christ I choose to forgive them for (name the specific offenses). I release their debt to me and I give it to You Lord. I forgive them and I ask You to bless them in Jesus' name. Amen.*
- Next, identify, renounce and break all agreements (or lies) with the demonic (even if they are implied agreements) Renounce and reject any teaching from or submission and /or allegiance to any leader involved in the occult. Say: *"I renounce and reject any and all leadership and teaching of (name the occultic leader, practice, or belief.)*
- Renounce specific occultic practices. Say: *"Father God, I renounce any and all practice of (tarot cards, Ouija boards,*

black or white magic, crystals, candle magic, etc.) In Jesus' name, I ask You to wash away by the Blood of Jesus any and all effects made on me caused by these practices I pray. Amen."

- Break and sever all (ungodly) soul ties with any leaders, lovers, or spirits that came about through these occultic practices. Say: *"Father God, I lift up (name the person, or spirit) to You, and in the name of Jesus Christ, I break and sever all ungodly soul ties between me and (name the person, or spirit) in Jesus' name. Everything that has been transferred from (him/her, it) to me, I give back in Jesus' name, and everything that has been given to them from me I take back in Jesus' name. Forgive my sin and heal the damage created by this ungodly union and seal Your work by the Blood, in Jesus' name. Amen."*

- Have the person pray, asking Father God to forgive them for all their sins and to cover all their sins in the blood of Jesus. Then make a pronouncement of forgiveness over the person. Say: *"As a servant of the Lord Most High, - Maker of heaven and earth, I pronounce you forgiven in Jesus' Mighty Name. Amen!"*

- Then take authority over any occupying spirits (witchcraft, sorcery, Satanism, idolatry, hatred, lust, etc.) and command them to go in Jesus' name. Say: *"In Jesus' name I take authority over the spirit of (name the spirit) and I command you to go, never to return, in Jesus' name!"*

- At this point I like to call in angels to sweep God's temple clean. If there are any demons left, command them to go! Say: *Father God, I ask You to send Your warring angels to come and to sweep Your temple clean. Come, Lord, and remove all demons and all stumbling blocks from Your Son/ Daughter in Jesus' name.*

- Lastly, ask God to fill any and all places vacated with His Holy Spirit. Pray, asking God to fill this person to overflowing, and then ask God to seal His work in them by the Blood of Jesus

Deliverance was one of the primary spiritual weapons Jesus used against the devil in His earthly ministry. Everywhere Jesus went, demons were routed and darkness was dispelled. Remember that Jesus came to set the captives free, and that He has called every believer to do the same. It's true that some may be set apart for a special ministry of deliverance, just as there are some set apart for evangelism. However, just because we may not have an evangelistic anointing doesn't mean we are not called to share the gospel. Not having a special anointing in sharing the gospel does not get you off the hook to evangelize the lost. In the same way, God expects every mature disciple to be trained and equipped in all the weapons of spiritual warfare. This especially includes deliverance. Sometimes deliverance may require something a little extra. This extra something is called anointing. It comes as we seek to cultivate a deeper connection and intimacy with God. It is this deeper intimacy and focus that often comes to us through the discipline of fasting. Let's take a closer look at this powerful spiritual weapon of warfare in the next chapter.

CHAPTER 13

FASTING

"Then the disciples came to Jesus privately and said,
'Why then could we not drive it out?' And He said to them,
'Because of the littleness of your faith; for truly I say to
you, if you have faith the size of a mustard seed, you will
say to the mountain, Move from here to there,' and it will
move; and nothing will be impossible for you. But this
kind does not go out except by prayer and fasting."
Matthew 17:19-21

Verb
Fasting:
1. To go without food for a spiritual reason or purpose.

I started this book sharing a personal crisis that I had gone through. This was a desperate time in my life. I had just lost my girlfriend; I had been discharged from the Marine Corps, and was pending my start date for Bible College. My heart was broken, and I was hurting, confused and desperate for answers. So I decided that I would fast and pray for three days. I didn't want to be distracted, so I left home and determined that I would spend the next three days in my car in a nearby park. All I did for three days was call out to God and drink water. I lived in my car for isolation. I was unshaven, and I looked like a homeless person, but I was desperate for some answers, so I stuck it out. The park closed at ten o'clock at night, so I had to find a place where I could park my car so I could sleep for the night. I drove around Fountain Valley until I found a darkened church parking lot. I pulled in and found a quick spot to park for the night. About an hour into my rest I was abruptly awakened by loud tapping on the windshield and two bright lights in my face. The officers were loud and unfriendly. They ordered me out of the car, demanded ID, and asked me a number of who and what questions. They told me that a concerned church member had called, and that I needed to vacate the premises. When I asked where they expected me to go; they said, "Anywhere outside Fountain Valley." I left there and decided to spend my nights in busier, less conspicuous, store parking lots. My nights were neither comfortable nor restful, but I was determined to do this. My days were spent in the park, crying out to God for some relief from my emotional pain and the despair I was feeling. The pain that I felt was deep and raw. After three days of prayer and fasting. I went back to my mom's house. I cleaned up, and started to get myself ready for my first college semester.

I was very disappointed that I had not gotten the answers that I was looking for. What I did not realize at the time was that my period of prayer and fasting put into motion a number of things that became milestones in my life. That first semester: 1) I found a mentor, 2) I became part of a men's group, 3) I had a radical encounter with God that changed my life and, was baptized in the Holy Spirit, 4) I started receiving a deep healing in my life, 5) I was delivered from demons, 6) I began experiencing God's power, 7) I started praying for others and seeing them healed! The whole school year was absolutely incredible, like nothing I had ever experienced –ever! My point is, I'm convinced that it all came about in answer to my three days of prayer and fasting in the park.

Fasting for Breakthrough

Fasting is a great spiritual weapon of warfare because it connects you to God in a way that brings about spiritual breakthrough like nothing else. Prayer and fasting is what brings our flesh into subjection to the Spirit. It crucifies our soulish nature and connects us to God in a deeper, more profound, way. Prayer and fasting resensitize our spirit and makes us more sensitive to the Spirit of God. It puts us in the Father's lap. It is this intimacy that lifts our faith and gives our prayers a greater impact. Prayer and fasting is a devoted period of time whereby we focus on drawing near to God for a spiritual purpose. Prayer and fasting is not for making God a genie in a bottle. It's about finding His will for a given situation and not so much about accomplishing ours. However, if our heart is right, and our will lines up with God's, we can be sure that he will give us the breakthrough we desire when we fast and pray.

Jesus in Matthew 17:19-21 indicates that it is fasting that gives us the breakthrough in prayer. When the disciples asked why they could not drive out the demon, Jesus told them that the reason was that their faith was too small. He didn't say that they had no faith. Yet he goes on to say that this kind only comes out through prayer and fasting. Now some may argue that what Jesus says in verse 21 is not contained in some manuscripts. However, I think we need to consider that Jesus himself practiced fasting. Jesus also taught his followers that **when** you fast you should not put on a gloomy face like the hypocrites do (Matthew 6:16). Jesus never says **if** you fast, He only says **when**, implying that all His followers will fast at some point in their walk. It's important to realize that Jesus directly links faith level to fasting and prayer. It's faith that brings the miracle. It's faith that brings the deliverance or the healing. It was fasting that gave me the spiritual breakthrough for my healing and started an all-out transformational renewal in my life during that season in college.

There are many good books on the subject of fasting. One author encourages his church to do a twenty-one day fast at the beginning of each year. My wife, Lori and I took this pastor's advice and tried this, and we've made it a practice ever since. Now more of our family has started to participate with us at this time of year. We've all received breakthrough in answer to prayers as a result.

When we all wanted to go as a family to Haiti on a short term mission's trip, we didn't know how it would happen. For my wife, my son, my daughter, and I to go would cost us $7200.00 round trip. There was no way we could do it, but we sensed God was in it. So we informed family and friends about what we were doing, and we fasted and prayed. For a while it seemed nothing was happening. Then after a few weeks, we started to receive checks. Sometimes cash was given. Twenty dollars here, fifty dollars there, sometimes forty came in, sometimes one hundred dollars came in. It was amazing! I was blown away! People began giving to us so generously that by the time we came to our deadline we had the total amount plus enough left over to feed the family on the way there! God is truly incredible!

Fasting has given me other breakthroughs as well. I was also pressing in to God for direction in ministry when he told me to write. It was definite when he spoke to me the fourth time! Apart from speaking to me directly about writing a book, God also gave me a word through two other prophetic individuals and by speaking to my wife about it. That answer and the confirmations that followed is what gave birth to the book you are now reading. In addition to the breakthroughs in prayer we found that fasting was beneficial for a number of other reasons. Having had high blood pressure for some time, I found after completing the fast that my blood pressure was perfect. The various health benefits were a fringe blessing. Besides cleansing our body from all the toxins our bodies store up, we learned that it strengthened our immunity and gave us more resilience to sickness. With the customary weight loss, our energy level improved significantly once our fast was over. I felt better, and my mind was clearer. I think the overall health benefits alone made our fasting worthwhile.

Our flesh can often cloud the voice of God with its impulsive demands on our time. There always seems to be more pressing issues that need our attention like our agendas, our wants, our desires and even our addictions. When the flesh is in charge, the only thing that matters is what we want. In this spiritual state the voice of God can be muted or silent all together. Fasting is the Lord's reset button. Fasting is what resets everything back to zero. It refreshes and restores everything; everything seems flush after a fast. As we put to death our natural desires, the Spirit is able to speak to us without distraction. Our stomachs may growl and scream out in protest, but our spirit comes alive with a new vitality, a new sensitivity to God's voice and presence. Fasting helps us to dial down and enables us to discern God's voice and movement. The end result is that our faith is increased, and we become more effective as we become increasingly dependent on the Holy Spirit for direction and guidance in ministry.

I hope that I have stirred your interest in this most overlooked spiritual weapon in the Christian's arsenal. There are many great books on the subject of fasting. I have only touched on it briefly to bring some awareness of fasting's power to bring about spiritual breakthrough in the believer's life and greater effectiveness in spiritual warfare in general. Fasting is only one of many tools the believer has available. In the next chapter we will look at some spiritual weapons that I have found to be extremely effective in ministry for helping to set the captives free.

CHAPTER 14

BREAKING CURSES

It is probably the opening of King Tutankhamun's tomb that has become the most well-known of curse legends. In 1922, Howard Carter led a team of archaeologists to open the pharaoh's tomb. Shortly afterwards, a number of VIPs were invited to view the tomb as well. The curse legend began to gain momentum and credibility as the various members and friends of Carters team began to die very untimely and unusual deaths over the course of the next seventeen years. From 1922 to 1939, twelve members and associates of Carter's team died, including Carter himself. One died from a mosquito bite infection, others died from fever, one was shot, another smothered in his sleep, still another poisoned, two died from malarial pneumonia, another committed suicide, and one died from "mysterious circumstances." I don't know that any of them knew Christ or had any belief in the supernatural, but many people in general both then and now are skeptical when it comes to curses and such.

For those who have no belief or experience with the supernatural, much of what I am about to say may seem fantastic. However, I am not addressing unbelievers, I am addressing believers. For this reason, I am not going to try and prove that curses are real. I am going to write presuming that if you are reading this book, you already know the power of the supernatural. Many who come for ministry are affected by curses, not even realizing that they are being subjected to a curse in the first place. The believer today needs to be aware and equipped to break the power of curses in the authority of Jesus' name. There are three types of curses that the believer needs to be equipped to confidently deal with. I will describe each type of curse and then give you the process I use to break the power of that particular curse. It's good to know that curses are easily broken because *greater is He that is in you than he that is in the world* (1John 4:4).

TYPES OF CURSES

WORD CURSES

The first kind of curse is the common "word curse." Back in chapter eight I talked about declarations and decrees. The point I was making is that words can have the power to effect change in a person's life. Just as God has given mankind the power to bless with his tongue, mankind can also bring down curses as well. Nowhere is this more vividly illustrated then when a parent berates, belittles and puts down their kid at some sporting event as the parent seeks to "motivate" their child to perform better. That parent may have good intentions, but their condescending tone and their harsh words can serve to curse their child with far- reaching consequences. Word curses impact a person when they receive that word into their spirit. Word curses can come from any number of sources including parents, teachers, coaches, siblings and, of course, peers. Words are sometimes charged with spiritual power and intended to do damage. Sometimes words or phrases are spoken over and over again to a person until that person begins to internalize the lie.

These curses can come through name-calling or labeling. This is most commonly witnessed on the grade school campus as kids will often bully and pick on one another. Words like fatso, weirdo, stupid, ugly, geek and slowpoke, can have a far reaching effect on an individual's self-worth when they internalize these words spoken to them repeatedly.

Even one careless word spoken by someone significant to that person can be damaging. Parents probably have the most power to impact their kids whether for good or for bad. One word from a parent can have a devastating effect on a child growing up. This is because God has given parents the unique ability to speak directly into the spirit of their child. One thoughtless word from a parent can have a radical impact on a child's sense of self-worth and value, altering their self-perception. This in turn, can serve to sabotage relationships, future successes, and even health. Word curses can impact children and adults alike. Whatever the circumstance, word curses can be changed by cooperating with the Holy Spirit to break their power. Here is a model you can use to break the power of a word curse over a person:

HOW TO BREAK WORD CURSES

1. When I minister to a person suffering from a word curse, I help them to first to identify the curse or lie they believe. Once they identify the lies they believe, I lead them through a simple prayer process to break the word curse affecting them.
2. First, I'll find out if that person needs to forgive the one who has cursed them. If they need to forgive anyone, I'll have them repeat after me.

3. *Father God, I choose to forgive (name the person) for cursing me by saying (fill in the blank of the specific words). I release their debt to me and I give it to You, Lord. I ask You to bless them in Jesus' name.*

4. *Father God, I renounce the lie that (I am never going amount to anything, etc. etc.) and I confess the truth that I can do all things through Christ who strengthens me.*

5. After that I pray over the person: *Father God, I take authority over this lie that (George will never amount to anything), and in the mighty name of Jesus Christ I break the power and the hold that this curse has had on (George) and I render it powerless and ineffective in Jesus' name! I break the power and the hold of any and all demons associated with this curse, and I render you powerless and ineffective against (George) and I command you to leave, never to return in In Jesus' name. Amen!*

OCCULTIC CURSES

The next kind of curse is an occultic curse. Occultic curses are curses that come intentionally through spells, incantations, hexes, potions or some other kind of ritual curse involving witchcraft. Sometimes curses will be placed on an object and given to an individual. The pharaoh's curse would be considered an occultic curse placed on an object. In this case, the object cursed was pharaoh's tomb itself. God understood the serious consequences of possessing the accursed or "devoted things" when He warned Joshua and the Israelites to *keep away from the accursed things so that you don't bring about your own destruction* (Joshua 6:18). It goes on to say however, that the Israelites acted unfaithfully because one man, Achan, son of Carmi, took some of these things the Lord had forbidden. The result was that Israel was defeated and fled from their enemies. Moreover, thirty-six men were killed by the men of Ai (Joshua 7:4-5). The only way things could be turned around for Israel was for them to purge the evil that had come into their midst.

> *"And it shall be that the one who is taken with the accused things shall be burned with fire, he and all that belongs to him, because he has transgressed the covenant of the Lord, and has committed a disgraceful thing in Israel"* (Joshua 7:15).

As Christians we are under a covenant of grace. *"For Christ redeemed us from the curse of the law having become a curse for us, for it is written, cursed is everyone who hangs on a tree"*(Galatians 3:13). As Christians we are no longer under the curse. The curse is broken. However, many believers still experience and live in subjection to curses. Why is that? It is because of demonic entities that still occupy. If you still believe the curse or lie spoken over you, if you are in agreement with the enemy, or if you are passive and have failed to take back ground from the enemy, he will continue to occupy and afflict you as though the curse is still in effect. Demons generally don't just give up and vacate their host voluntarily. They have to be expelled and kicked out. We enter our "promised land" (the fullness of the blessing of Christ) through battle. The good news is that Christ has already given us authority, power, and victory over the devil. All we need do is take back what is rightfully ours.

If a person is an unbeliever, then they need to be saved by putting their faith in Christ. This allows them to come under the blessing of God in Christ Jesus.

Sometimes people without knowing better have come into contact with objects that are cursed and some even wear them on their person without knowing or understanding the ramifications of wearing such an item. Examples would be things like rings, necklaces, or amulets dedicated to various other religions or occultic temples of worship. It is always good to know where these things come from. Some souvenirs from other countries have been devoted to other gods and have spiritual attachments that can affect the owner of the object when they get home, whether they are a believer or not. Jewelry that has been dedicated to spirits or cursed in some occultic ritual and then sold in the marketplace gives the demonic grounds to afflict you if you own it or are wearing it. Hanging a souvenir mask on your wall may look cool, but it is an endorsement of what that mask represents if you are displaying it in your home. This gives the demonic grounds to afflict you and your family. Consider this when buying gifts abroad.

Another occultic curse happens when a person has come out of another religion or cult where they have submitted to the leadership or teachings of an occultic leader or leaders. This alliance or agreement with leaders or teachings can make the person subject to curses and can give the demonic grounds to attack and afflict. It can also allow curses to be placed on them by the leaders of such organizations.

HOW TO BREAK OCCULTIC CURSES

I once ministered to a man that I will call Ben (not his real name). He was a Christian at the time of our meeting, but he seemed very much oppressed. As he began to share some of his story with me, I learned that he had been involved in the occult for many years prior to becoming a believer. His involvements led to sexual ties with multiple persons within the cult including the leader. He had also confessed to being involved in a number of sacrifice rituals. His countenance was deadpan and he seemed emotionless. So I began to lead Ben through a prayer to break the power of any curses put on him because of the sin he committed while in the cult and also any curses put on him by others for leaving the cult. I told him to repeat after me:

1. *Father God, in the name of Jesus Christ I utterly reject and renounce any and all leadership and teachings of (name the cult leader or teacher). In Jesus' name I utterly reject and renounce any and all submission or connection to this organization, its leadership and following.*

2. *In the name of Jesus Christ I break and sever any and all soul ties to the following people (name the person or persons involved). Whatever I received from them, I give back, and whatever I gave, I take back in Jesus' name. I ask you to apply Your blood to my sin and to forgive and heal the damage caused by these ungodly unions in the name of Jesus.*

3. *Father God, I confess my sin before you, and I ask You to forgive my sin and idolatry. Forgive me as I forgive those who have harmed and sinned against me. Cover me and seal me with the blood of Jesus. Amen.*

4. I then say, *Father God, in the name of Jesus, I break, shatter and destroy all curses and conspiracies sent against (Ben) as a result of these sins and I pronounce him forgiven by virtue of Christ's blood, and I declare him righteous in Jesus' name. Amen!*

5. *I take authority over any and all demonic sources and spiritual powers of wickedness, and I render any and all*

assignments against him null and void in Jesus' name! I command you to leave and vacate (Ben). I command you to go, and I forbid you to return in Jesus' name. Amen!

6. Father God, I ask you to send Your holy angels to sweep Your temple and to remove all stumbling blocks and remnants of evil in Jesus' name.

7. Now fill (Ben) with Your Holy Spirit and flood his body, soul and spirit with the light of Your Presence in Jesus' holy name. Amen!

SEVERING BLOODLINE & GENERATIONAL CURSES

"You shall not make for yourself an idol in the form of anything in heaven above or on the earth beneath or in the waters below. You shall not bow down to them or worship them; for I am a jealous God, punishing the children for the sin of the fathers to the third and fourth generations to those who hate Me, but showing love to a thousand generations to those who love Me and keep my commandments."

Exodus 20:4-6 NASB

Another kind of curse is the bloodline or generational curse. The above passage in Exodus indicates that sin can have a generational impact on a family. Bloodline or generational curses are handed down from a person's family lineage and can come from the sins of our fathers, mothers, aunts, uncles, grandparents, or even a person's great grandparents. These generational curses are enforced by a demon that entered the family through the originating sin. This demon has the grounds to enforce the curse until such time as the curse is broken and the demon expelled. Even if a curse is broken, the demon may still be resident and enforcing the curse. Demons typically don't voluntarily give up their host. They have to be forced out. This is one reason many passive Christians continue to live defeated in some area of their lives. Our enemy may be defeated, but he is never passive. I say this because even if a particular curse is broken, it may be necessary to expel any demonic occupation for breakthrough.

Examples of Bloodline or Generational Curses

Bloodline or generational curses become easily identified when there is an obvious, unhealthy history of serial behavior repeated cross-generationally in one family. Generational curses are easily seen over the course of one's family lineage and history. Some of the more obvious examples of bloodline or generational curses are addictions of various kinds including alcoholism, physical or sexual abuse, divorce, mental illness, irrational fear, depression, fits of anger, violence, and even family illnesses such as specific kinds of cancer. The person who is so called "accident prone" may be contending with a curse. Habitual financial difficulty may be a spirit of poverty inherited by ones family lineage. These are just a few examples of bloodline or generational curses.

Why do bloodline or generational curses exist?

You may be asking why God would punish the children for the sins of the parents. To answer this question we first have to ask ourselves about God's intended role for parents. It was always God's intention for parents to cover and protect their families spiritually.

> God gives instruction to families under the old covenant, *"You shall therefore impress these words of Mine on your heart and on your soul; and you shall bind them as a sign on your hand and they shall be as frontals on your forehead. And you shall teach them to your sons, talking of them when your sit down in your house and when you walk along the road and when you lie down and when you rise up. And you shall write them on the door posts of your house."*
>
> Deuteronomy11:18-19. NASB

Under the new covenant, God's people are still commanded to instruct the next generation – to cover them spiritually!

God's word instructs spiritual leaders to cover and attend to their families so that their children grow up embracing the faith. Titus 1:6

As spiritual leaders, the older are to teach the younger what is good. Titus 2:3-6

God gave responsibility to the patriarchs and matriarchs of each family to teach and instruct their children in the ways of the Lord. When one or both parents sin against God by rebelling or embracing a lifestyle of sin, the spiritual covering intended to protect the children starts to break down and is eventually destroyed. This gives the demonic access to wreak havoc on the family, often for generations.

Consider the "ripple effect" that something like alcoholism has on a family as the children are denied the full-time attention and resources of that parent. The children are denied that parent's "best self" because alcohol has become an idol and the priority in the family. Consider the emotional abandonment they grow up with, the relationship problems, the difficulty with school, as worry begins to affect their concentration. Consider how their adult years are impacted as they become emotionally stunted and underdeveloped at the various stages of their lives. Emotional neediness often drives them to choose relationships that are somewhat less than healthy. How much will their overall potential be diminished? How susceptible will these children likely be to a world that is preying on them? Will they stand when faced with sin, temptation and lies? How much access to them will the enemy of their soul have? How much influence? Moreover, what kind of parent will *they* be someday? These questions underscore the critical need of a spiritual covering over ones family and its importance.

When parents fail to cover their children, whether for sin, rebellion, neglect or ignorance, it gives the demonic grounds and access that will always be felt for generations beyond its origin. God has given us the authority and the responsibility to protect our children and future generations by covering our families spiritually. That means being diligent to pray a covering over our marriages and our children. It also means teaching and instructing our children in the ways of the Lord and being watchful and aware of our enemy's schemes.

I love the movie "It's a Wonderful Life." I watch it a least once a year. It never fails to encourage and remind me of why I am here. In the movie, the father played by Jimmy Stuart falls on hard times and contemplates suicide when his guardian angel, Clarence, intervenes. Discouraged and dejected, the father makes a statement that it would have been better if he had never been born. With that comment, the angel Clarence obliges him and gives the father a rare sneak peek at what his town, family and friends would have been like had he never existed to influence them. In the end, the father is given the revelation of his own significance, his value, and the positive ripple effect that the impact of his life has had.

The message of this movie has great significance to me because of the positive spin that it gives on the ripple effect of our lives. As representatives of Jesus, He has given us authority to break and sever any curse that would affect our children and grandchildren. God has given us the power to destroy and cut off the enemy's plan for our marriages, our children, and our future generations for years to come.

HOW TO SEVER BLOODLINE OR GENERATIONAL CURSES

Here is one way to break generational curses. When I am praying for someone who I believe is being affected by a generational curse I always start by following these steps:

1. First, I help the person to identify the curse that may be influencing their life. This may be obvious after the initial interview.
2. Once we have identified the curse, I begin helping them to resolve any forgiveness issues. They must forgive those who have hurt them and sinned against them. Some may need to forgive God and repent for putting blame where it doesn't belong. Next, if necessary, they must forgive themselves. Have them say: *Father God, I forgive (name the person -s) for (state the offense). I release their debt to me, and I give it to You Lord. Forgive me for my*

unforgiveness as I forgive and release them. I also ask You to bless them in Jesus' name. Amen.

3. Then I lead them to break and sever all ungodly soul ties if necessary. Have them say: *Father God, I lift my (Father, mother, aunt, uncle, etc.) up to You, and in the mighty name of Jesus Christ I break and sever all ungodly soul ties from (name the person) to me and from me to them. All that was stolen from me I take back and all that was given to me I give back in Jesus' name. I ask You, Lord, to restore me, washed in the blood, and to heal any damage caused by the ungodliness of this union. In Jesus' name I pray. Amen.*

4. Next you want that person to break and sever the bloodline curse. Have them repeat these words: *Father God, I lift (name relative) up to You, and in the mighty name of Jesus Christ I break and sever the bloodline curse of (addiction, cancer, abuse, etc.) back to the 2nd, 3rd and 4th generations. I break, shatter, destroy and renounce this curse handed down through this bloodline, and I cut it off in Jesus' name. Amen!*

5. Now cast out the spirit responsible for enforcing that curse. Pray: *In Jesus' name, I now take authority over any and all spirits of (addiction, cancer, abuse, etc.) responsible for enforcing this curse, and I break your power in Jesus' name! I render your assignment over the bloodline of (name the person you are praying for) null and void in Jesus name! Go and don't come back! Amen!*

6. Now pray a blessing over that person and over any and all future generations coming from them. Say: *I bless (name the person) with (freedom, health, protection, etc.) and I bless any future generations coming from their bloodline. I thank You, Father, that they are under the blessing of Abraham, and that you are blessing both them and their children to the 2nd 3rd and 4th generations in Jesus' name. Amen.*

CHAPTER 15

BREAKING AND
SEVERING SOUL TIES

"For this cause a man shall leave his father and mother, and
shall cleave to his wife and they shall become one flesh."
Genesis 2:24

SOUL TIES

You may be wondering what is a soul tie? A soul tie is a
soulish/ spiritual bond between two people created by deeply
personal interaction. When we talk about soul ties, many
people think they only come about by means of a sexual
union, but that is not always the case. God intended soul ties
to be a good thing to promote unity and oneness between a
husband and a wife; yes, but soul ties are also formed between
parents and children, and are even formed in the context
of deep friendships. In 1Samuel 18:1 we read, *"Now the time*
came about when he had finished speaking to Saul, that the soul of
Jonathan was knit to the soul of David, and Jonathan loved him as
himself."(NASB) We see here that a deep friendship was formed
between these two god-fearing men as they identified with
each other's bold faith.

CAUSES OF UNGODLY SOUL TIES

Soul ties were intended to be a good thing, and they are in many instances. However, sometimes ungodly soul ties are formed by very personal and damaging events that can become a spiritual gateway for the demonic. Sometimes what is thought to be a generational curse is, in fact, an ungodly soul tie. Ungodly soul ties are usually formed by a sexual union that is outside of God's intended purpose. This intended purpose is strictly limited to the covenant of marriage between a man and a woman. Any time two people have sex outside of what God has sanctioned in His word, it is outside His blessing and protection, thus giving the demonic grounds to afflict and oppress. However, ungodly soul ties can also be formed by trauma and acts of violence. It is through such events that the demonic can gain access to afflict and torment a person.

Ungodly Sexual Unions

We live in a day and age where sex is treated very casually. The millennial expression of "hooking up" has replaced the 1960's version of "free love." Young people today are talking about having "friends with benefits." The reality is that most people today perceive casual sex as nothing more than a fun, recreational activity. What many fail to realize is that sex is a profoundly spiritual event that never leaves the participants the same. As mentioned in Genesis 2:24, the two actually do become one flesh. In other words, there is an exchange that is more than physical. It is a tethering together of two human souls that can never be undone apart from a miracle of God. Casual partners may go their separate ways, but they carry something from that other person that will forever remain.

On a spiritual level, there is a transferring of spirits which can be potentially disastrous in ones day-to-day life. This is especially true if the other person has any kind of demonic attachments or occupants. An ungodly sexual union gives the demonic a free pathway into the other person's life, most of the time without their knowledge.

Trauma and Violence

Another source of an ungodly soul tie is trauma, such as sexual abuse, childhood molestation, or rape. Even physical or emotional abuse can become the source of an ungodly soul tie. It is sometimes minimized when someone recalls a parent yelling and verbally abusing them as a small child. Nonetheless, verbal abuse can have a lasting imprint on that person's soul. I am convinced that even physical fights and altercations at times can lead to ungodly soul ties. Any event involving another person that is traumatic and deeply personal can become the source of an ungodly soul tie.

Vows, Oaths or Pledges

Soul ties can also be made by making vows, oaths or pledges to a leader such as the leader of some cult, false religion or fraternal secret society in the person's past. Though they have become a Christian, there still is some spiritual connection that continues to allow the enemy to harass the former member, now a believer in Jesus. Some have thought they made the oath or pledge all in good fun, but in spirit realms you are held to your words. This vow or oath to a leader can be a soul tie that gives the demonic access to the person seeking help and gives the enemy grounds to afflict and oppress. God takes your oaths and vows very seriously. That is why Jesus said, *"And I say to you that every careless word that men shall speak, they shall render account for it in the day of judgment."* Matthew 12:36 NASB

In Matthew 5:33-37 (NASB) Jesus was teaching regarding oaths and vows saying, *"Again you have heard it was said to the people long ago, 'Do not break your oath, but keep the oaths you have made to the Lord.' But I tell you, do not swear at all: either by heaven, for it is God's throne; or by Jerusalem, for it is the city of the great King. And do not swear by your head, for you cannot make even one hair white or black. Simply let your yes be yes and your no be no; anything beyond this comes from the evil one."* The evil one would seek to have you make an oath to some leader to trap you in your words and have grounds to oppress you. If you have made an oath in the past, then renounce the oath to that leader at once in Jesus' name, and be set free from it!

These are just some of the ways soul ties can be formed in a person's life. Thankfully, by God's mercy, grace and power, ungodly soul ties can be broken and severed, giving that person their freedom back and cancelling any spiritual assignment that came through the soul tie. As you follow this prayer model, being sensitive to the Spirit of God, you will discover that severing ungodly soul ties can have profound results at times.

Let me say that what we are seeking to do is to break and sever only the **ungodly** soul ties in order to preserve God's work and intention for that relationship. This is typically done when the soul ties involve family members. Occasionally, I encounter people seeking ministry who have had a connection to an individual or a number of people with no redeeming factors. In other words, the "relationships" from start to end were ungodly. In such cases, I break and sever **all** soul ties –period. This is done with the prayee's understanding and approval, of course. Here is a simple prayer model that I typically use in such ministry situations.

HOW TO BREAK AND SEVER SOUL TIES

1. Start by clarifying the ungodly soul tie and its effect on the person. I explain the process and ask the person if they are willing to have God sever those ungodly soul ties. If they are willing, I proceed.
2. Then have them resolve any forgiveness issues. Once we have identified the ungodly soul tie, I begin helping them to resolve any issues where forgiveness is needed. They must forgive those who have hurt and sinned against them. They must forgive God and repent for putting blame where it doesn't belong. Next, if necessary, they must forgive themselves. Have them say: *Father God, I forgive (name the person -s) for (state the offense). I release their debt to me, and I give it to You, Lord. Forgive me for my unforgiveness as I forgive and release them. I also ask You to bless them in Jesus' name. Amen.*
3. I will then encourage them to repent and renounce any sin if necessary. Have them say: *Father God, I am sorry for my participation in any sin involving (name the person). I repent of (name the specific sins) and I renounce these sins in Jesus' name, and I ask You Father to cover these sins in the Blood of Jesus. Thank You for Your forgiveness, Lord.*
4. Then I lead them to break and sever all ungodly soul ties where it is necessary. Have them say: *Father God, I lift my (Father, mother, aunt, uncle, boyfriend, girlfriend, etc.) up to You, and In the mighty name of Jesus Christ, I*

break and sever all ungodly soul ties from (name the person) to me and from me to them, all that was stolen from me or given away, I take back and all that was given to me I give back, in Jesus' name. I ask You, Lord, to restore me washed in the Blood, and to heal any damage created by this ungodly union in Jesus' name. Amen!

5. Now cast out any and all afflicting or oppressing spirits that have gained access to this person through the ungodly soul tie. Pray: *In Jesus' name, I now take authority over any and all spirits of (abuse oppression, torment, etc.) responsible for (name the affliction), and I break your power in Jesus' name! You have no authority here. I render your assignment over (name the person you are praying for) null and void in Jesus' name! Go, and don't come back! Amen!*

6. Finally, I like to finish the ministry session by praying for God's healing and blessing over the person. Say: *Father God, I bless (name the person) and I ask you Lord to seal your work by the blood of Jesus. Holy Spirit, surround (name the person) and place Your hedge of protection around them. Brood over them, Lord, and continue to heal and restore their heart to wholeness in Jesus' name. Amen!*

CHAPTER 16

GOD'S COURTROOM

"Now there was a day when the sons of God came to present themselves before the Lord, and Satan was among them. And the Lord said to Satan, 'From where do you come?' Then Satan answered the Lord and said, 'From roaming about the earth and walking around on it.' And the Lord said to Satan, 'Have you considered my servant Job? For there is no one like him on the earth, a blameless and upright man, fearing God and turning away from evil.' Then Satan answered the Lord, 'Does Job fear God for nothing? Hast Thou not made a hedge about him and his house and all that he has on every side? Thou hast blessed the work of his hands, and his possessions have increased in the land. But put forth Your hand now and touch all that he has, and he will surely curse Thee to Thy face.' Then the Lord said to Satan, 'Behold all that he has is in your power, only do not put forth your hand on him.' So Satan departed from the presence of the Lord."
Job 1:6-12 NASB

There are some things that we will never understand this side of heaven, like why does Satan get access to God's presence in the first place? Why does Father give him an audience? Why does He even grant him a conversation? Why is it that Job is allowed to be caught in the middle as a helpless pawn in what seems like a cosmic grudge match?

All we can do is speculate that God, in His wisdom, has a grander purpose, a greater purpose, and uses the devil and his minions to test our hearts, bringing hard times upon us when we stray to bring us to repentance as in the case of the apostle Peter (Luke 22:32). Or perhaps God allows the enemy to afflict to keep us from being puffed up and prideful as in the case of the apostle Paul's thorn in the flesh (2 Corinthians 12:7). Perhaps it even goes beyond that. Perhaps God uses Satan to teach us how to stand in our faith. Maybe these tests are to teach us how to fight spiritually so we can learn to exercise our spiritual authority and take our rightful place as co-heirs with Christ (Romans 8:17). Maybe God allows evil to come against us to teach us how to defeat and conquer it. Perhaps God has been spending the last 2000 years setting us up to walk in victory so that we can learn how to destroy darkness. It's the Job experience that will always be a mystery, which will always beg the question, "Why God?" Then again, perhaps *why* is the wrong question to be asking!

Dan and Shirley (not their real names) came for prayer. They appeared to be a high powered couple, intelligent and very competent. They owned and ran several large businesses. They were very serious about their faith; they were always very active in ministry and gave to a number of charities on a regular basis. In the course of the last two years they had experienced several major financial losses and setbacks, including a pending law suit. Neither of them was aware of any sin in their lives or anyone that they needed to forgive. We asked the Holy Spirit to reveal any secret sins in their lives that they could possibly be unaware of and the Lord was silent on the matter. Once we had done everything we could to troubleshoot their long string of mishaps, and I was sure that we had covered all the bases, I concluded that they had entered into a "Job Experience."

A "Job Experience" is when a person has pulled out all the stops to get right with God, yet has no apparent relief from their circumstances. To be clear, I am not talking about prolonged trials because of one's own irresponsibility, sin, or mismanagement. In those cases, trials might be expected. A Job experience is when a very serious believer comes under severe trials and attack over a prolonged period of time with no apparent reason for it. In the case of Dan and Shirley, they had already confessed any sin they were aware of; they had forgiven their enemies, fasted, prayed, and sought intercessors. They had remained faithful in giving with their finances and yet nothing seemed to bring the relief they were seeking. They had exhausted their spiritual knowledge as to what to do, and they were desperate.

As in Job's case, there are occasions when the Lord grants the enemy permission to sift, test, and humble us in order to keep us dependent on Him. Why these trials are sometimes prolonged over extended periods of time I can only guess. What is interesting in the Biblical examples of Job, Peter, and Paul is that each one of these men was exceptional in their own right. Job was a successful land owner and very wealthy. Peter was a very independent commercial fisherman and had a very lucrative business. Paul was a very learned and educated individual; moreover, from the scriptures we know that Paul was a mover, a very headstrong individual who almost succeeded in destroying the church before the Lord had turned him around. Because of these examples, it is likely that the Job experience is the exception rather than the rule, and that it is usually reserved to keep the very gifted, successful and self-sufficient person humble and dependent on God.

Some trials are no doubt longer than others. In the case of the prolonged "Job Experience" I have no personal story, but I had heard of a couple that was having similar repeated setbacks like Dan and Shirley. This couple prayed, looked for any sin in their lives and were not consciously aware of any; they fasted and prayed to no avail, and nothing changed. In fact, things only got worse. Eventually, their finances were completely tapped. Their circumstances brought them to the point where they were about to be homeless when they decided to go to God's courtroom to bring their petitions before the Lord. Now I might add that they didn't go about this lightly. They came before the Lord with much fear and trepidation, understanding that doing this could make their circumstances even worse. Understand that they were not approaching God as Father but as their Judge, asking Him to render a verdict. However, they did it anyway because they were desperate. First, they demanded that Satan be present before God. Then they came before God's courtroom with their petitions in hand and made their petitions before the Lord, but only under the blood of Jesus. Otherwise, no one could stand before God. When it was all said and done, they waited. Eventually over the course of time all their petitions were answered. God had rendered the verdict in their favor! Their finances were restored. They moved into new housing, and the enemy finally abated.

Now, let's get back to Dan and Shirley. It was only with the knowledge of this story that I had gotten the idea to lead them before God's Courtroom. I explained carefully that we would be approaching God as the Judge of the universe. Satan would be the prosecutor, and Jesus our defender. Before we began,

I had them write out all their petitions. Once they had done this, court was in session.

HOW TO COME INTO GOD'S COURTROOM

First I prayed, *Lord we humbly come before You as Judge of the universe. Let it be known that we only come before You on the basis of the finished work of Jesus Christ and by His shed blood on the cross. It is by the shed blood of Jesus that we come before You to request a hearing before You and our accuser.*

We also make a demand that Satan present himself before You this hour.

We also humbly present our following petitions before You.

Present Your Petition:

At this point, I had Dan and Shirley presented their petitions. Being unfamiliar with this approach, they proceeded with reverence and caution.

Over the course of the next half hour Dan and Shirley made their case before God. They explained that they both felt that they had been called to a ministry of giving. It was in their hearts to support specific ministries, and they were both sure that God had led them to support these ministries. They went on to explain that Satan for the last two years had ravaged their finances and had drawn out a long litigation process. They said that much of their time, energy, and resources were being wasted in court. They went on to say that their effectiveness had been radically diminished and their troubles had prevented them from being as effective as they wanted to be. They ended by asking the Lord for relief against the enemy.

I finished the session by saying, *Lord, You know all the circumstances of Dan and Shirley. You know what the enemy has put them through and how Satan has dragged this on and on for two long years. Enough is enough, Lord. As our Judge, we ask You to render a verdict between Dan and Shirley and their accuser Satan. Let Satan bring his arguments if he has any before You now. We now wait by faith for You to render a verdict. In Jesus' name. Amen.*

I let Dan and Shirley know that if they needed any future prayer they could return any time and I would be happy to pray for them. The good news is that they have not returned. My hope is that God rendered the verdict in their favor. To this day I don't know what became of that couple. This I do know, however: our God is gracious and compassionate, abounding in love, and is a God who relents from sending calamity. This had been my only use of God's courtroom, and I thought it to be a useful weapon in the believer's arsenal. I included it at the end of this chapter to equip the believer with another resource to use in the most extreme circumstances.

CONCLUDING THOUGHTS

I was just visiting a house church in my area not long ago. There, I met a young lady who shared that she had been delivered from drug addiction and healed of schizophrenia. She now leads mission teams and is in fulltime ministry. As I reflect on her testimony, I am reminded of the fact that she was healed, delivered and helped by believers who were disciples of Jesus and fully equipped with the spiritual weapons to set her free. In other words, her life was changed because some believers understood who they were in Christ and what was available to them. They were consequently equipped to help change the course of her life. This is just one example of the mission of Christ being fulfilled in the life of an individual.

The mission of Christ is grand and can be overwhelming. Evil seems to permeate every corner of the world, but God has equipped believers with the spiritual weapons and the resources to not only defeat darkness, but also to establish His rule and reign in our communities and in the world! We can't just sit back and play church anymore! We as the church must begin taking an aggressive posture toward spiritual darkness. If the whole church understood what is available to us as believers in Christ, together we could change the world! Darkness could not stand. It would be no match. For too long the church has been passive, taking a defensive posture, held captive like scared sheep. Why are Christians afraid of the supernatural? God reversed the curse of Adam through Jesus

Christ and has given back our dominion over the earth! Our enemy is spiritual. Let's go after the enemy and take back what rightfully belongs to us as sons and daughters of God! Let's plunder Satan's kingdom and push back darkness by loving people and covering our communities! Let's stop the mass shootings in our communities! God has given us the means to take dominion.

God has given us not only the authority, but also the spiritual weapons necessary to demolish the enemy's camp throughout our country and the world. The riots, mass shooting sprees in our schools and workplaces, and the unrest throughout the world reveal the very thin veil between civilized society and total anarchy. It is our influence as believers that preserves society and hold things together!

We are sons and daughters of the King of all kings. As representatives of Jesus, we are part of a royal priesthood. This status gives us access to a spiritual arsenal that has devastating power against evil. We as believers in Christ can stay the enemy's hand. We can dismantle demonic strongholds, demolish fortresses, tread on scorpions and serpents, and break curses. We can bind and loose. We can release blessing and be the dispensers of God's love, healing and grace. What an honor!

It is complacency that comes by affluence and the desire for a comfortable and easy life that has seduced many into a life of compromise. This has unfortunately left many victimized by an unseen enemy that has established a foothold in their lives and the lives of their children and households. For this reason it is time to arm ourselves and commit ourselves to the battle that Jesus calls each of us to. It's time to take back the ground that was lost! It's time to push back and displace darkness! It's now time to enter our promised land! The fullness of the blessing of Christ will be ours only when we learn to win the battles within. When we win the battle over ourselves we will start to experience breakthroughs in our marriages and our families. Then we will take back our homes, our workplaces and communities.

Weapons were meant to be used. Weapons will do no good if left in the arsenal. We must learn to access and deploy them. Our failure to do so will result in a loss of personal freedom and influence over the culture, and a perceived sense of irrelevancy. Moreover, lost souls and future generations are at stake. The reality is that you have authority over all the power of the enemy! Do you believe that? Does your life reflect that reality? It can, now that you know what's available to you. Now you can make a difference. Now you know how you can change things. Now you know how you can begin suppressing the influence of evil.

Now that you have finished this book, congratulations! You have just become a more effective weapon for the kingdom of God, and here's why:

- You should now have a greater awareness of your positional authority in Jesus Christ. God has given us authority over all the power of the enemy. You have the power to tread on scorpions and serpents, and nothing shall by any means injure you.
- You are also now familiar with the full spectrum of spiritual weaponry made available to you through the finished work of Christ. Like the tool box of any master workman, God has equipped His church with spiritual weapons, specialized for any occasion. We are each called to deploy these weapons to destroy darkness and to further the kingdom of God, bringing light, healing and freedom to every sector of society.

- Moreover, you now have a working knowledge of how to bind the strong-man and shut down the demonic in your sphere of influence, in your marriage, in your household and in your school and workplace. Consequently, your neighborhood, school and workplace can be safer places because you are there covering them.
- It also means that you have at least a starting point regarding the various tools for entering into the ministry of Jesus, to begin healing the sick, binding up the brokenhearted, and setting the captives free. If you haven't started already, I want to encourage you to begin entering into the practice of healing the sick. It is incredibly fulfilling when God begins healing people through you!

Now that you've been made aware of these spiritual weapons, I want to encourage you to begin deploying these to protect your marriages, families and workplaces. Try getting together with other believers to study these weapons together and to begin exercising them. Experiment, and then compare notes. The purpose of this book is to equip believers to walk in victory and to defeat darkness. God's heart is that every believer would walk in the fullness of the blessing of Christ and enter their promised land.

As I said earlier, Marines train for war. They train so that when the day of battle is upon them they know what weapons are available to them and how to use them. They train so that when they are in the heat of battle they don't back down or quit. They train to win at all costs. My hope is that you will commit yourself to learning the weapons of our warfare, becoming proficient with them, and using them to build a better world!

Ministry Information

David Jacques is a licensed minister with RAIN, Resurrection Apostolic International Network and ministers with his wife Lori at the Ventura Healing Rooms.

Contact David Allan Jacques for speaking at training seminars and conferences.
E-Mail: Unseenpwr62@gmail.com

Printed in the United States
By Bookmasters